CITY OF THE DEAD

THEBES IN EGYPT

FRONTISPIECE
Harvesting grapes
(TT 261).

CITY OF THE DEAD
THEBES IN EGYPT

LISE MANNICHE

THE UNIVERSITY OF CHICAGO PRESS

FIGURE 1 (page v)
Scribe taking notes
(TT 261).

FIGURE 2 (pages vi–vii)
Drawing by *camera lucida*
of a scene in TT 113.
From Hay MSS 29822,
124.

The University of Chicago Press, Chicago 60637

British Museum Publications, 46 Bloomsbury Street,
London WC1B 3QQ

 Published 1987
Printed in Great Britain
96 95 94 93 92 91 90 89 88 87 54321

Library of Congress Cataloging-in-Publication Data

Manniche, Lise.
City of the Dead.

Bibliography: p.
Includes indexes.
1. Tombs—Egypt—Thebes (Ancient city) 2. Thebes (Egypt: Ancient city) 3. Art, Egyptian—Egypt—Thebes (Ancient city) 4. Excavations (Archaeology)—Egypt. 5. (Egypt)—Antiquities. I. Title. II. Title: Thebes in Egypt.
DT73.T3M36 1987 932 87-5022
ISBN 0-226-50339-9

Designed by Sharyn Troughton

Set in Monophoto Ehrhardt 11/12pt
and printed by BAS Printers Limited,
Over Wallop, Hampshire

To the memory of Dr Ramadân M. Saʿad
Chief Inspector of Upper Egypt

CONTENTS

ACKNOWLEDGEMENTS
Page ix

1
THEBES WEST: CITY OF THE DEAD
Page 1

2
THE BEGINNING
Page 17

3
THE EIGHTEENTH DYNASTY
(1575–1335 BC)
Page 29

4
THE RAMESSID TOMBS
(1308–1087 BC)
Page 64

5
THE LATE PERIOD
(1087–525 BC)
AND THE END
Page 84

6
REDISCOVERY
Page 93

7
MODERN TIMES
Page 115

BIBLIOGRAPHY
Page 131

LIST OF THEBAN TOMBS AND
THEIR OWNERS
Page 132

INDICES
I GENERAL II ANCIENT NAMES III MODERN NAMES
Page 147

ACKNOWLEDGEMENTS

I am much indebted to the Egyptian Antiquities Organisation for allowing me access to the Theban tombs over the past many years and for its willingness to accommodate my wishes. My thanks extend in particular to Dr Ahmed Kadry, President of the Egyptian Antiquities Organisation; Mr Mohammed es-Sughayir, Chief Inspector of Upper Egypt; Mr Mohammed Nasr, Chief Inspector at Qurna; and Dr Mohammed Saleh, Director of the Egyptian Museum in Cairo and formerly inspector at Qurna.

To Dr G. T. Martin I owe a debt of gratitude for having taken time from his own busy schedule to read the book in manuscript. And to the person to whom this book is dedicated I am indebted for having conveyed his enthusiasm for and concern about the monuments of the Thebans, which were in his care for only too short a time.

The photographs for the frontispiece, figures 1, 5, 7–8, 11–13, 18–19, 25–27, 29, 31–37, 41, 44, 46, 49, 54, 60–63, 69, 71, 82, 85–86, 89, 91, [100] and 101 were taken by the author, many of them being converted from colour slides to black and white prints by Dr Adam Bülow-Jacobsen, Copenhagen, to whom I am truly grateful for having carried out the task at short notice.

Figs 14, 45, 48, 56, 58–59 are due to the late Dr Ramadân M. Sa'ad, who took the photographs at my request some fifteen years ago.

Figs 2–4, 10, 16, 39, 50–51, 53, 55, 65–67, 76, 84, 87–88 and 102 are based on or directly reproduced from Hay and Burton MSS in the British Library. I am indebted to the Library for permission to publish them.

Photographs provided by museums have been acknowledged in the captions.

FIGURE 3
Birds in the papyrus thicket from Antef's tomb (TT 155); the scene is now destroyed. From a tracing by Hay MSS 29851, 387–8. Courtesy the British Library.

I

THEBES WEST: CITY OF THE DEAD

The ancient city of Thebes was split in two halves by the River Nile; yet it remained 'The City', and it was the religious capital of Egypt during the New Kingdom (1575–1087 BC). The sight which greets the traveller today has little in common with a busy metropolis. The town of Luxor on the east bank of the river boasts a number of large modern hotels to accommodate the increasing quantities of tourists, but beyond the pretty promenade Luxor remains a small provincial town. The blessings of modern civilisation: an airport; a railway station; a hospital; a veterinary clinic; secondary schools; and administrative offices distinguish Luxor from its twin town on the other side of the river. The crossing by motor boat takes barely five minutes, but the two banks are a world apart. All attempts at connecting the two by means of a bridge have hitherto come to nothing. The village of Qurna on the 'other side' remains separate, its isolation being broken only by the bus loads of

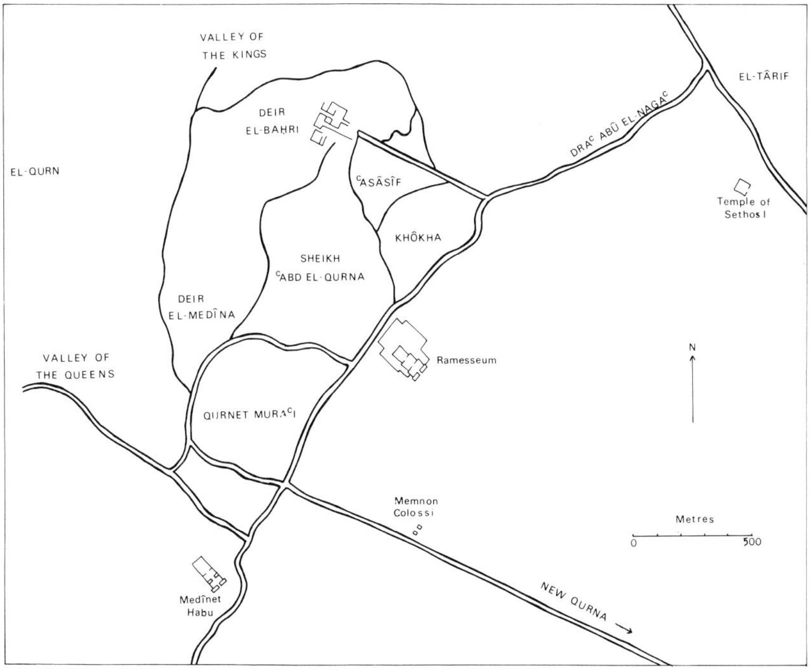

FIGURE 4
Map of the Theban necropolis.

tourists coming over in the morning and going back to Luxor before lunch. The afternoon is the time to absorb the spirit of Qurna.

The area takes its name from the peak of the mountain el-Qurn ('the horn'), the pinkish orange cliffs rising above the fertile land to one side and desert valleys to the other. The name is now loosely applied to the entire stretch of land between the cliffs and the fields, but the conglomerations of houses have their individual names. To the north, disappearing behind a hill and with its towering mosque, is Draᶜ Abû el-Nagaᶜ ('Abû el-Nagaᶜ's arm'), last call before the road branches off to the left to the Valley of the Kings and to the right to the mortuary temple of Sethos I, the 'palace of Qurna' as it was called by the early travellers in the nineteenth century. At Draᶜ Abû el-Nagaᶜ the inhabitants work in 'alabaster factories', skilfully imitating their ancestors in cutting vases of soft calcite ('alabaster') under the porches of their houses. Dust from the drilling makes the road into a glittering milky way. The village comes to an end where the hills retreat to form a wide basin under the steep cliffs. Queen Ḥatshepsut, who saw Qurna in its virgin state before most of the buildings now standing had been put up, chose this dramatic setting for her own mortuary temple, as had a king hundreds of years before her. The flat area to the south of the causeways, where the only notable standing edifice is a huge brick arch of an ancient tomb, is the ᶜAsâsîf. Towards the fields the ground rises to form a small hill with a handful of houses scattered around it, appropriately called Khôkha ('the peach'). Further to the south the houses again move up the hillside at Sheikh ᶜAbd el-Qurna, named after the Muslim saint whose tomb crowns the hill. The mound of Qurnet Muraᶜi, which rises majestically with its pretty houses as one approaches from the river, completely hides from view the last settlement to concern us here, the village of Deir el-Medîna ('convent of the town'), no longer inhabited by the living.

The villages, and the treasures they shelter, are the subject of the present book. But we must not forget to mention the splendid ruins

FIGURE 5
View of the Theban necropolis, looking North East from Sheikh ᶜAbd el-Qurna.

of the temples in the plain where the desert meets the cultivation, and the tombs of the kings and queens in two separate valleys in the desert, where they hoped, in vain, to rest undisturbed in perpetuity.

As we shall see in a later chapter, the people of Qurna used to live in the tombs. The caves in the rock provided a convenient shelter for animals and humans alike, and high up in the cliffs they were an excellent vantage point in times of trouble. Needless to say, if the walls of the tomb were decorated with paintings or reliefs they suffered greatly through deliberate or accidental destruction. Expropriations of the tombs were undertaken by the beginning of the present century and continued until some sixty years later all tombs with decoration had been vacated. Some houses still possess a niche with a painting in it, duly protected by an iron grille; in others the decoration is so sparse that the house's use as a storeroom has been approved. So although the people no longer live inside the decorated tombs, they maintain their residence in the houses built among them.

One understands why the people of Qurna are reluctant to move. Being above the ground away from the humid fields makes all the difference during the hot summer months, and the caves are cool and convenient. Provided with a wooden door, they make a safe locker; with

FIGURE 6
Tombs and houses at Qurna, painted by W. Prinsep (1794–1874). Courtesy Martyn Gregory Gallery.

a low wall of stone they are turned into a comfortable shelter for a donkey and a few sheep and goats.

The houses on the hillside are built of mudbrick and consist of a few rooms and a courtyard with a roof of palm branches. The cooking is done on an open fire or on a kerosene stove. Water is brought on donkey back or carried on the head from the water tap by the road. Down here the houses are larger, tall and square with decorative pointed cornerstones and small windows with mosquito nets and wooden shutters, in appearance not at all unlike the houses of the ancient Egyptians. Most of them are well kept, freshly plastered with Nile mud or washed with blue, yellow or white. Electricity has been introduced and with it some refrigerators and television sets. But most houses are still without these conveniences, and the school children do their homework sprawled on the ground under the street lamps.

It is difficult to gauge how the inhabitants regard their remote ancestors and the heritage they left them. In the early days of tourism the tombs were a source of income; digging for antiquities was a profession. Christianity and Islam never worked for the preservation of early pictorial representation. It was not until the second half of the previous century that educated Egyptians realised that the past was worth conserving, not just exploiting, and there was a long way to go before rural areas, and Qurna in particular, adopted this point of view. By the beginning of the present century local dignitaries began to fund restoration work, and soon it was understood that unless the monuments were looked after, the tourists would have no reason to come to Qurna. The standing monuments provide jobs and customers, and the people of Qurna feel special because they have so much to offer. Provided the proper credentials, in other words tickets for the monuments, are in order, the visitor is always made welcome.

Not so many years ago the dedicated tourist could enter almost any tomb he wished. The keys were with the *gafirs* (guards) of the different sections of the necropolis, and provided the key had a number attached to it and the tomb could be found, all doors were made open. It so happened that it was too easy to gain access, and certain tombs suffered. It was therefore decided to leave only a selection of tombs open to tourists, each with a guard assigned to it. Most visitors never have the time to see more than a few anyway. These choice tombs are now in immaculate order and it will be an unforgettable experience for those who enter a Theban tomb for the first time.

The remaining tombs are accessible to students and scholars with a serious purpose. For their protection the entrances to many tombs have been blocked with walls of stone in addition to the iron doors. Tombs in the plain and among the houses are apt to become covered in dust and debris, whereas those on the hillside are less affected.

Although a great deal of work has been carried out in the tombs and many of them have been published, they remain an inexhaustible source of information about life in ancient Egypt. In addition, most of them

FIGURE 7
Opening TT 249. The tomb is in the plain at Sheikh ʿAbd el-Qurna and has been protected by a wall of stone and mud plaster over the iron door

are works of art, though time and man may have treated them badly. The masterpieces among them are well known from books on art and archaeology. For the present publication we have attempted to include reliefs and paintings which are less familiar to the general reader. Each representation has something to offer either from an iconographic, religious or linguistic point of view, and each little fragment is part of the jigsaw puzzle of Egyptian civilisation, from which so many pieces are missing.

FIGURE 8
Food supplies for life in the Hereafter (TT 253).

Although the tombs reveal a wealth of details about life in ancient times, they are above all tangible evidence of the funerary beliefs of the people. These are complex, for several options, never mutually exclusive, were available for life in the Hereafter. Birth and death are the most radical changes man can experience during the course of his life. The Egyptians preferred an unchangeable state of affairs, or at least a change that followed a familiar pattern like the change of the seasons. Death was regarded as a change, not an end. Contrary to what is generally believed the Egyptians did not envisage life in the Hereafter as an exact replica of life on earth. The sources are very explicit when it comes to describing the means by which the Egyptians hoped to ensure a continuation, but less so in explaining the kind of existence they expected, and their preoccupations may therefore appear to be chiefly concerned with basic needs like food and drink and clothing. These primeval beliefs were never discarded, but they developed into more sophisticated ideas. From the moment the Egyptians had learnt to express themselves in writing, we are told that the food and drink placed in the tombs are not meant for the body of the dead person, but for his *ka*, his dynamic force, his personality. Experience must have told them that the body itself is fragile even when made to look indestructible through mummification.

The *ka* lived in the tomb. The earliest tombs imitate houses, including such mundane details as lavatories. The relatives brought meals to the tomb and placed them at the 'false door', through which the *ka* was believed to communicate. The custom of burying the body in a subterranean chamber and decorating the upper rooms with reliefs or paintings was begun in the Old Kingdom and lasted until the last dynasty of pharaohs. The pictures had a life of their own inside the tomb, playing

the part of their real counterparts if the relatives ignored the needs of the tomb owner and his *ka*. Once these basic needs had been arranged, the tomb provided the starting point for the deceased when he departed in his various guises. Some were more academic than others, but they all had one aim in common: to enable the dead person to partake of eternity and to move a step forward in the cosmic cycle of birth-life-death-rebirth.

FIGURE 9
A false door with the tomb owner kneeling at either side (TT 343). Photograph taken in the 1920s. Courtesy University College London.

To some eternity was an existence among the fixed stars on the northern sky. They remained apparently static, while other stars went their mysterious ways. In theory, the deceased would be able to transform himself into anything he desired, from a lotus flower to a swallow. A popular choice was a *ba*, a bird with human head. By becoming a *ba* the deceased was able to fly out from his tomb and mingle with the

FIGURE 10
The tomb owner and his wife transformed into *ba*-birds (TT 19). From Hay MSS 29851,163.

living. People were never quite sure what to make of the *ba*-birds in their midst, for they were known to be able to cause grievous harm if they felt so inclined.

Osiris was a central figure in the world of the dead. Having once ruled

FIGURE 11
Funerary scenes showing (1) Osiris adored by the tomb owner and his wife, and offering bringers; (2) the coffin and funerary equipment being carried in procession; (3) scenes from the ritual of the Opening of the Mouth; (4) the voyage to Abydos (TT 139).

the earth he had passed to become king of the dead after his brother had murdered him. In the Old Kingdom any reigning king became transformed into Osiris when he died. His successor on the throne was thought of as Horus, son of Osiris, until he himself died, whereupon he became Osiris. The original Osiris was believed to materialise in the sprouting grain as part of the perpetual cosmic cycle. With the collapse of the Old Kingdom and the king as god supreme, the Egyptians maintained their belief in Osiris to the extent that they themselves wished to identify with him. Osiris was now not only the name of the revered god; it became a title applicable to those who had passed the test. By identifying with Osiris any Egyptian had the opportunity to be part of the eternal cycle and to live through the grain in the field, the river swelling and receding, the moon increasing and decreasing.

An alternative option for eternity was to follow the sun in its daily course across the sky, to be on board the day boat and the night boat of Rē, the sun god himself, and to be born anew every morning. Immortality took the rhythm of the cosmos.

The Hereafter was not a complete void; it had a shape, however vague. The concept of a marsh landscape is reminiscent of a state of affairs which the Egyptian of Pharaonic times can hardly have experienced. Hence the fanciful description: 'I know the field of rushes. Its walls are made of metal; the grain in it is four cubits high, the ear one cubit and the straw three cubits.' This text inspired the representations of the deceased and his wife harvesting oversized grain on the walls of some tombs. But originally the fields were rushes growing in water. It is not only in Egypt that a passage over water is obligatory on the journey in the Hereafter. The river was the source of the water, yet subsoil water also appeared when the farmer dug a hole in the field. The fields of rushes had to be located somewhere underground, near the source of the water, and the kingdom of Osiris as well. The entrance to this promised land was the tomb in the cliffs.

After the appropriate period of preparation in the embalming house the deceased was ready for the funeral procession to the tomb. One tomb owner left a description of his burial as he wished it to be performed (TT 110):

> 'Fair burial comes in peace when your seventy days are completed in the house of embalming. You are placed on a bier and drawn by young cattle. May the ways be opened by sprinkling of milk, until you reach the entrance of your tomb chapel. May the children of your children be collected in an unbroken circle and weep in affectionate mood. May your mouth be opened by the lector priest and your purification be performed by the *sem*-priest. May Horus adjust your mouth. May he open for you your eyes, your ears, your members, your bones, so that your natural functions are complete. May the spells be read for you and a ritual offering, your heart being with you, the heart of your earthly existence, and you come in your former person as on the day on which you were born. May your beloved son and the friends

FIGURE 12
Priests opening the mouth of the mummy (TT 260).

be marshalled for you, performing the benediction of the ground and the burial of that which the king has proffered in the vault of the West. May there be a delivery of gifts for you as for the ancestors. May the forefathers come to you with chants and may the favours of the god to one he loves not come to an end for ever and ever.'

This is a remarkably precise statement about the first steps on a journey from which no one had returned. The same tomb owner had taken explicit precautions for provisions in the Hereafter, and he ventured into a description of a state of affairs about which he could only guess. He invokes the gods and makes an offering to them:

'that they may grant thousands of invocation offerings consisting of bread, beer, oxen, fowl, bags and strips of linen, incense, unguents, offerings, delicacies, oblations, green herbs of all sorts, everything good and pure, everything good and sweet, such as heaven yields, earth creates, and the Nile brings out of its cavern, respiration of the sweet breezes of the north wind, draughts of the watering place of the river, existence under various forms, wanderings throughout the fields of rushes, putting on of clean clothes, finest sheets, or white linen, the use of cosmetics and unction with fine oil at a feast in heaven, the sight of the orb of the sun when it arises on the horizon of heaven, the reception of cakes offered on the altar of the Lord of Plenty, a place among the followers of the sun god in the western mountain, ascension to heaven and admission to the underworld, without being netted(?) along with the stars, the assumption of the form of a living *ba*-bird. May it settle on its trees and take advantage of the shade of its sycomores. May it perch on the apex of the pyramid. May the mummy be durable and the sarcophagus not lacking to it, so that it rests in its abode.'

It is on reading a text like this that one is thankful for the literacy of the Egyptians. Without it their concepts would have remained totally obscure.

It is a curious fact that most Theban tombs were never completely finished. A medium-sized tomb could probably have been cut, plastered and painted within the time required for the corpse to be embalmed, if the most expensive and time-consuming method of embalming was employed. Even if an Egyptian had been caught unawares without having made arrangements for his burial, it ought to have been possible to complete a tomb in time. Reluctance on the part of relatives to keep the work going once the master of the house had died is not a very convincing answer either, although it may actually be the true reason. One is left with the impression that completion of the tomb was deliberately delayed in the hope of postponing the date on which the burial facilities would be required.

Tombs were left in various stages of completion from roughly hewn chambers to tombs with just a few lines of hieroglyphs wanting. This does not explain the cause, but it provides an excellent demonstration of how the tombs were cut and prepared.

A rough passage was made into the rock until the intended final length was reached. A line was marked on the ceiling by dipping a cord in red paint and stretching it from the entrance to the focal point, marking the axis of the tomb. The transverse hall and any subsidiary chambers were cut at right angles to the axis, leaving masses of stone where pillars were intended. The shaly rock came off easily by using hard stone mauls with pointed or chisel-shaped cutting edges. If harder rock was encountered chisels or adzes of bronze were substituted. Hard patches would include boulders of flint which were impossible to cut through. They were either cut out in one piece and the cavity filled with mud, stones and plaster, or they were left protruding from the wall, sometimes being incorporated into the decoration.

In order to ensure perfectly straight walls the surveyor marked out the distance from the red axial line in each section of the tomb by drilling holes along the wall until the bases of the holes were equidistant from the axial line. Completed holes were marked with a touch of black, and the stonemasons could go ahead on their own. The roof was levelled off by drawing a horizontal line on the walls and measuring upwards.

To a certain extent the quality of the rock decided whether the final decoration was to be in relief or painting. At the bases of the hills at Qurna the rock is of a quality suitable for cutting relief, whereas higher up it is too friable. But sometimes even good stone was painted only.

The firm white limestone tempted a few painters to lay the colour directly on the surface without suitable preparation with the result that the colours became dulled or scaled off.

The proper way to prepare a wall for painting was to cover the rock with a layer of mud plaster up to 20 cm thick, mixed with chopped straw to bind it. This in turn was given a coat of gypsum. On drying, the mud plaster often pulled away from the rock making a slightly undulating surface, which was kept in place only because it was wedged in between the floor and the ceiling of the tomb. Mudbricks were used to fill large holes and even to build whole walls and vaulted ceilings, notably in the village of Deir el-Medîna, where the rock is particularly shaly. Pieces of dried donkey dung, being very light were occasionally used to fill holes in the ceiling, which were then plastered over with mud. In one instance the large nuts of the *dôm*-palm served the same purpose.

As the hand marks show, the mudplaster was always applied with the fingers, but for the final coat a float or a brush was used. The layer of gypsum varies from about 3 cm to just a thin coat. A pore-filler consisting of lime carbonate and size was used on top, or the colours would have become absorbed in the gypsum.

For the tomb to be sculpted the rock face needed to be dressed very carefully, first with a chisel, then with an adze. Cracks in the surface

FIGURE 13
The artist's first sketch and a grid (TT 87).

were filled in with gypsum, and a thin coat or wash was laid on the wall to conceal the flaws. If a large area was found to be faulty a block of stone was wedged in as a substitute. The design to be carved was outlined in black paint and the background of the figures cut down to a depth of a few millimetres with a fine-edged chisel. An abrasive was used to remove the chisel marks. The square edges of the reliefs were rounded off with a knife or hand-chisel, leaving smooth and even cuts. Minor details were then modelled, such as hands, feet, ears and prominent muscles. In some tombs of the Ramessid period the relief is sunk so shallow that the modelling inside the bodies is almost level with the background. The finished relief was occasionally covered with a thin layer of gypsum, in which case the colours stood a better chance of surviving.

All reliefs were meant to be painted, but because proper preparation of the surface was so often omitted the colours have vanished, and we are left with reliefs of almost classical starkness. In other cases the paint appears to have been scrubbed off in modern times, perhaps to achieve this very effect. Where colours remain, it is often where the relief was not cut in the rock, but in plaster, a technique popular in Ramessid tombs. The carving had to be carried out before the plaster had hardened. When damp and freshly set it can be worked with a hammer and chisel, but when it is quite dry it tends to chip off. The Egyptians must have developed a method of applying plaster to a limited area at a time, although there is no sign signifying how this was achieved.

The palette of the painter was restricted, but within his limitations he gave Egyptian painting its true characteristics. Tradition weighed heavily on his shoulders. A colour code had been laid down at an early stage, and during the three thousand years of Egyptian civilisation it hardly ever varied. Black, white, red, yellow, shades of blue and green, and occasionally pink and grey were all the colours the painter needed. Minor natural variations occur within each colour but did not affect the colour concept as such, and to go to the trouble of identifying one or the other shade with its exact replica on a modern colour chart is absurd for most purposes.

The source of most of the pigments was close at hand. Black consisted of soot scraped off cooking vessels, or ground charcoal. White was either chalk or gypsum readily available from the cliffs. Red oxides of iron and yellow ochre can be picked up in the desert in the form of lumps encased in sand. When broken up and ground they produce the rich pigments which have lasted so well on the walls. Orpiment was an additional source of yellow. It occurs naturally, but not in Egypt, and it was imported, probably from Persia. In spite of the fact that yellow ochre could be collected in the neighbourhood, some painters preferred the use of orpiment in the tombs.

Blue and green were the colours which were difficult to obtain in that they needed a certain amount of preparation. The principal blue pigment was an artificial frit consisting of a crystalline compound of silica, copper and calcium. The pigment has been reproduced in modern times by heating together fine sand, copper carbonate and salt. Green was an artificial frit like blue, or powdered malachite was used, a natural ore of copper which occurs in the eastern desert and Sinai. Both light and dark shades of blue and green were used, not without discrimination. Pink was not unexpectedly a mixture of red ochre and white gypsum, whereas grey was produced by mixing gypsum and charcoal.

When the pigments had been ground they were mixed with a paint vehicle. Black, red and yellow would adhere to a wall even if just mixed with water, but a more permanent result was obtained by adding gum or eggwhite. A colourless varnish was sometimes used to bring lustre to the colours, but over the years it has turned yellowish. Beeswax was occasionally used to the same effect.

While the stonemasons were busy cutting through the rock at one end of the tomb and the plasterers followed in their footsteps, the outline-draughtsman moved in as soon as the first wall was plastered and dry, or, if the tomb was to have decoration in relief, he followed as soon as the wall was smooth. His work was the same in both cases; to lay out the design on the walls and draw the figures in ink. Any painter could fill in the colours and the details. The initial sketches showed the true master.

There is some evidence to suggest that the draughtsman worked from a pattern book which he would perhaps show to a prospective customer, who would then order 'one banquet scene', 'one fishing and fowling', 'one showing me in my important office as such and such', and so on. Pattern books for paintings have not survived, but scrolls with architectural drawings are known. The evidence for their existence is more than suggested by the curious case of Wensu and Paḥeri. Wensu was scribe of the accounts of grain at Thebes; Paḥeri was an important official in the town of el-Kâb, some fifty-five miles south of Thebes. Wensu had his tomb cut in the rocks at Draʿ Abû el-Nagaʿ and decorated with a number of conventional scenes in the best style of the mid-Eighteenth dynasty painting. Paḥeri naturally chose to have his tomb made in the cliffs near his native town of el-Kâb. Apart from the fact that Paḥeri's duties also included supervision of granaries far beyond the district of Thebes, there is nothing to suggest that the two men had anything to do with each other, were it not for the curious fact that certain scenes in their tombs are absolutely identical. That Paḥeri's tomb is carved in relief and that of Wensu is painted shall not concern us here; it only goes to show how closely related the two techniques were.

The only way in which the design so many miles apart could be so similar is by copying a common source. The contemporary royal tombs of Tuthmosis III and Amenophis II show beyond doubt that the painter had consulted a scroll of papyrus while he worked. Not only has the decoration in these two royal tombs the unmistakable characteristics of sketchy papyrus design; but the text was damaged, notably at the beginning of the scroll which was the most vulnerable when the scroll was stored. The scribe who copied the text left blanks where his scroll was broken, or he wrote 'found damaged'.

The painters of the private tombs probably used similar scrolls to guide them; but it would be interesting to discover why the tombs of Wensu and Paḥeri are a unique case. One would expect more tombs to be alike or even identical, if pattern books were in general use.

The ancient craftsman would be able to copy a drawing from one medium onto another freehand. But the grid had long been found useful to give the figures their correct proportions. It was applied to the walls by means of a string dipped in red paint, and it would vanish under the successive layers of paint.

The subjects depicted on the walls of the tombs change and develop through the different periods, as will be demonstrated in the following chapters. But in enthusing over these beautifully decorated tombs we must not forget that they represent only a fraction of the burials in the Theban necropolis. Others were in undecorated pits for instance. Thebes was one of the only two real cities in ancient Egypt and must have been densely populated. All these people died and were buried. The official number of decorated tombs now stands at about 415 to which must be added about fifty decorated tombs which were known to the early travellers in the nineteenth century but the exact location of which is now unknown. But there is evidence to suggest that the number of decorated tombs was much higher.

This evidence is in the shape of cones of clay, some 10–15 cm high, the circular bases of which have a stamp of hieroglyphic signs giving a name, a title, and sometimes a family relationship or a short inscription. These 'funerary cones' have puzzled scholars since they were first

FIGURE 14
Funerary cones assembled in TT 151.

brought to notice some 160 years ago. They have been interpreted as 'mummy labels'; 'boundary stones' to mark the territory of a prospective tomb owner; dummy offering loaves or pieces of meat; 'visitors' cards'; dummy roofing poles; or as a purely decorative element, for it was realised by some that the cones were originally placed as a frieze above the entrance to the tomb, set in the wall with the circular end visible. A recent suggestion takes into consideration that the circular shape is identical to the shape of the sun's disc and would perhaps allow the person whose name it carries to partake in the solar cycle.

Funerary cones are chiefly a Theban phenomenon, although some of the people named on them had occupations which took them elsewhere. It is a curious fact that no cones have a definite connection with Deir el-Medîna, the section of the necropolis reserved for the workmen cutting and decorating the tombs of the kings. In time they occur from the Eleventh dynasty to the Late Period (2000–600 BC), but the cones which do not belong to the New Kingdom can easily be isolated, either because they are uninscribed (the early cones) or through an inscription which dates them with certainty to a period later than the New Kingdom. These cones, which are not from the New Kingdom, are very few in number compared with the rest. Among the New Kingdom cones the majority can be assigned to the Eighteenth dynasty, which gives us a very large group of cones and therefore persons, who were known to have lived within a limited period of time and to have made arrangements for a tomb of which the cones formed an element.

Through the names and titles it is not difficult to match owners of funerary cones with owners of tombs. If one takes as a criterion a minimum of two common denominators, like name and title, as proof of identity, it is possible to identify about eighty cone owners of the New Kingdom with as many tomb owners. This leaves us no less than about 325 tombs for which no cones have been found. On the other hand the number of cone owners to whom no tomb has yet been attributed is more than four hundred.

Each tomb owner had upwards of three hundred identical or similar cones. Before we consider the possibility of adding four hundred tombs to the list of decorated tombs, we must consider whether it was possible to insert one's funerary cone in someone else's monument. Some cones have a woman's name only preceded by 'his wife'. Virtually no women are known to have had tombs of their own. There certainly seems to have been no place for unmarried women in the world of the decorated tombs. The only person in modern times to have seen a row of inscribed funerary cones *in situ* was Rhind in the 1850s, and although he was a keen observer, he does not reveal whether the cones he saw carried the same inscription. Uninscribed cones of Eleventh dynasty date have also been discovered in their original setting. It remains a possibility that each example of an inscribed cone represents one decorated tomb, and in that case the number of decorated tombs would be at least twice the number of tombs known at present.

2
THE BEGINNING

In the days before Thebes began to rise to glory it was a provincial town like many others, far removed from the capital of Memphis in the north. This is naturally reflected in the surviving monuments: the tombs. The court claimed the best artists, and the tombs of the high officials at Gîza and Saqqâra are those which attract attention. In those days Thebes was confined to the east bank in the area where the temples of Karnak now tower over the palm trees. The inhabitants were buried immediately opposite on the west bank of the river. This ancient necropolis is situated in the angle formed by the modern Fadlîya Canal and the road leading from the river to the temple of Sethos I, the area called el-Ṭarif. People had lived here since prehistoric times, for the tombs are built on top of remains from the Naqâda II civilisation (*c.* 3300–3000 BC) followed by a layer which in turn is covered by a layer containing stone tools and seals of First dynasty date.

As the cemetery is in the plain and not in the mountain, the architecture of the tombs reflected these conditions and followed the tradition established in the north: they were of the so-called *mastaba* type consisting of a subterranean burial chamber reached through a shaft, with a superstructure of mud bricks around an earth core in the shape of a brick bench (Arabic *mastába*), in which was incorporated a chapel with mudplastered and white-washed walls. These *mastaba* tombs have been dated to the Fourth dynasty (around 2500 BC). Bodies were buried on their backs with the heads to the north, resting on a stone slab, and they were accompanied by storage jars with food and cosmetic vessels. Only two tombs of this type have been recovered at Thebes, and both had been re-used and rebuilt. It looks as if they were part of a larger cemetery which has since vanished under tombs of a later date.

It remains a mystery where the governors of Thebes of the Fifth dynasty were buried. Scattered finds prove that they did have tombs, but there is otherwise a complete blank for this period. In the Sixth dynasty the centre of the necropolis had shifted to the area of Khôkha. Five tombs are representative of this dynasty. They are cut in the rock and decorated with paintings on plaster or with reliefs. One or several burial chambers reached through sloping passages house the dead, while a pillared decorated chapel was cut into the hillside above. No uniform plan had as yet been adopted, but one of the tombs shows the transverse hall, later so characteristic. The method of preparing the walls for decoration had been established: the rough walls were covered with mud mixed

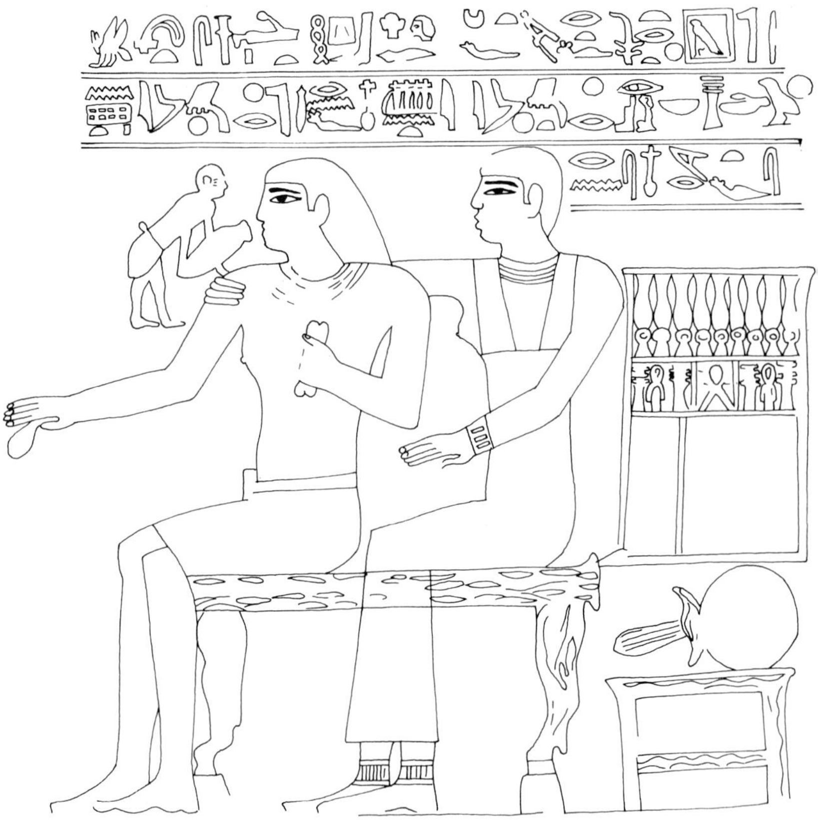

FIGURE 15
An Old Kingdom tomb owner and his wife (TT 405).

with straw and given a light cream wash, though some walls needed only the wash, which was in this case a dark grey colour.

The scenes depicted include large-scale representations of the tomb owner and his wife with heaps of offerings before them and rows of people bringing more; slaughtering; grinding corn, baking and brewing; fishing and preparing the catch; the granary and agricultural activities; all subjects which have a direct bearing on the sustenance of the *ka* in the Hereafter. In two tombs we have representations of metal work, which must reflect the importance of this industry on the tomb owner's estate. At the funerary banquet entertainment is provided by female harpists and dancers performing among other things a mirror dance where the point was to reflect one's hand or a hand-shaped object in a mirror held in the other hand, the dance being associated with the cult of the goddess Ḥatḥor.

It is interesting to find in these early tombs two subjects of which we shall have occasion to speak later: the symbolic voyage to Abydos, and the tomb owner fishing and fowling in the marshes. A third precursor of a scene shown in some New Kingdom tombs is the representation of the bedroom.

The owners of these five tombs of the late Old Kingdom held the highest provincial offices. Two (tombs no. 186 of Iḥy and no. 405 of Kheti) were governors of Thebes; another (tomb no. 185 of Senioḳer) was 'hereditary prince and divine chancellor'; Unasankh (tomb no. 413) was governor of the South and overseer of the granaries; whereas the fifth, whose tomb has no number and whose name is disputed, was 'overseer of the priestly phyles of the nome'. We are thus dealing with the cream of Theban society at the end of the Old Kingdom, just before the collapse which led to a period so disorganised that Egyptologists could think of no other name for it than the First Intermediate Period. People lived and died at Thebes during these 120 years or so of famine and feuds, but they left no tombs, and they remain anonymous.

By 2134 BC the situation began to change with the rise to power of a Theban family several members of which bore the name Intef. One of them eventually called himself King of Upper and Lower Egypt and sat on the throne for more than fifty years, thus providing a focus for

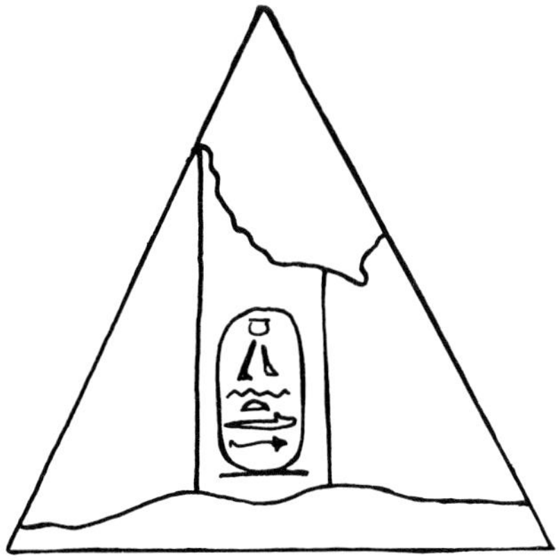

FIGURE 16
The pyramidion from the tomb of Antef, found in the previous century. From Hay MSS 29848, 38.

stability and prosperity. He and his successors made their tombs at el-Ṭarif where the inhabitants in the Fourth dynasty had built their *mastabas*. As was the custom the court officials followed their sovereigns and crowded their tombs around the three large tombs of the Antef kings. The tombs here are of a characteristic type generally called *ṣaff* tombs (*ṣaff* in Arabic meaning 'row' (of holes)). A shallow courtyard was sunk into the desert plateau, the chapel being cut into its rear walls. The chapels are quadrangular, the roof being supported by one or two pillars. Shafts or corridors contained the burials. Numerous stelae were found in the area which had originally been inset in the façade of the tombs. The royal tombs at least were crowned by a pyramid.

After the Antef kings, rulers who bore the name Mentuḥotp again shifted the centre of the necropolis to the south. Mentuḥotp II built his magnificent funerary monument under the vertical cliffs at Deir el-Baḥri: a pyramid resting on two pillared terraces with a tree-lined causeway leading up from the valley. The monument was completed by his successor. Mentuḥotp had his burial chamber cut immediately below the pyramid, the entrance being through a sloping corridor opening up

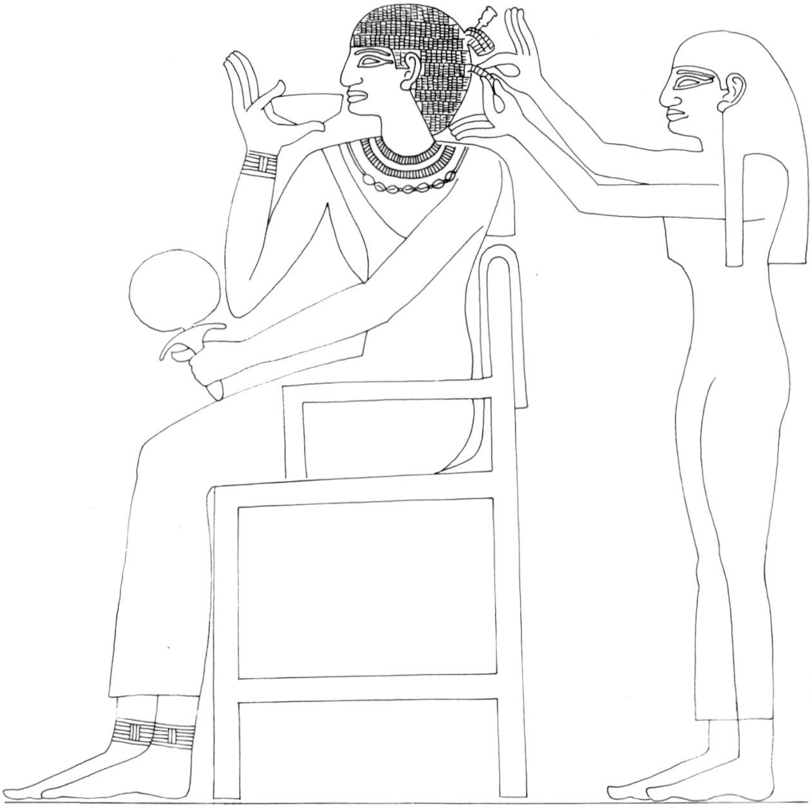

FIGURE 17
A maid using a hairpin to arrange the curls of Queen Kawit's wig. From the sarcophagus of the Queen in the Cairo Museum.

in the forecourt. Alternative arrangements for a burial were made in the courtyard behind the pyramid. Members of the royal family were buried in chapels nearby. Among the six young women one was just a child; another was 'unique royal concubine', Kemsit, whose burial chamber is decorated with reliefs of her receiving offerings and being attended by her maids.

Princess Nofru had her tomb excavated in the cliffs just outside the temple. The upper part of the tomb takes up the themes of decoration seen in the tomb of Kemsit: offering bringers and toilet scenes in relief, while the burial chamber is decorated with painted funerary texts and objects almost like the inside of contemporary coffins. Several hundred years later the tomb was built over when Queen Ḥatshepsut laid out her mortuary temple, but a tunnel enabled the curious tourists of the Eighteenth dynasty to visit the tomb of the princess. Numerous graffiti on the walls bear witness to the antiquarian interests of the ancient Egyptians. The decoration in sunk relief is of superb quality, but now very fragmentary.

The members of the court and high officials cut their tombs in the cliffs above the temple. The governors and viziers, the chancellors, a great steward, a custodian of the king's harim, sealbearers and a custodian of the bow were laid to rest up here. In the cliffs to the south, on the slopes of Sheikh ʿAbd el-Qurna, we find the majestic tomb of Dagi, who had no less than twenty-eight titles, the highest ranking being governor of the town and vizier. His tomb (no. 103), much later re-used as a Coptic church, was decorated with fine limestone reliefs, but like most Middle Kingdom wall decoration it is now smashed. The chapel is a portico with six pillars. Apart from offering scenes and the voyage to Abydos the subjects depicted concern activities of daily life: gardening and harvesting grapes; spinning and weaving; storing grain; baking; metalwork; fishing; tending cattle; in brief, daily chores on a large estate which we shall soon meet again in a different medium. One of Dagi's own personal duties has been included: as vizier he was in charge of supervising the recording of treasure.

The cliffs to the north shelter the tombs of other high officials, commanding a breathtaking view of the countryside. In the tomb of Kheti, the chancellor (no. 405), brick steps lead to the rock cut façade of the tomb, which originally had a huge wooden door. A long corridor leads directly to a painted chapel inside, where a statue of the tomb owner once greeted the visitors. Those with evil intentions were deceived by two false crypts, for the real burial chamber with painted decoration of offerings and funeral equipment lies at the end of another passage deep down. The sarcophagus was buried under the floor slabs, but in spite of all these precautions the chancellor was not allowed to rest in peace. The reliefs in the upper corridor suffered a strange fate: they were broken up and used to make stone vessels, leaving only fragments of the original decoration to suggest the delicate reliefs of hunting scenes, fishing and fowling, and dancing, all destroyed for the sake of the manufacture of insignificant dishes sometime towards the end of the Pharaonic period.

Of the tomb of Ipi, the vizier (no. 315), little decoration has survived, but the tomb yielded two interesting finds: one was a cache of embalming materials which had been left over when the mummy of the tomb owner had been prepared. The other was the archives of Ḥekanakhte, one of Ipi's mortuary priests, which were found in a hole of the passage. Through these personal papers we gain an unusual insight into daily life and its various problems which were committed to writing some four thousand years ago.

The chancellor Meketrēʿ chose a central position for his tomb (no. 280) to the south of the royal mortuary temple. With its large courtyard and portico of octagonal columns it was impressive, decorated inside with painted reliefs of which, needless to say, hardly any remain. But the tomb has gained fame because of the finds made in it. In the burial chamber were discovered more than 1200 model tools and weapons as well as the remains of the chancellor's coffin. Tomb robbers had deprived Meketrēʿ of all chance of survival, but in one respect he outwitted them. In a chamber under the floor he stored a miniature copy of his estate: his villas, stables, slaughter house, granary, weaving workshop, kitchen,

FIGURE 18
View of Meketrēᶜ's tomb with the Late Period tombs of the ᶜAsasîf in the background.

fishing boats, pleasure boats and servants, who would all go on producing for him in the Hereafter and provide nourishment for his *ka*. These wooden models are the most perfectly and beautifully carved specimens ever found in Egypt. Models as such went out of use by the end of the Middle Kingdom when scenes on the walls were considered sufficient.

The inspector of Meketrēᶜ's storehouses was a man called Waḥ. He chose to be physically near his master after death as well, and he was granted permission to have a tomb cut in the courtyard of his master's

FIGURE 19
Two of the Cairo models from the tomb of Meketrēʿ: carpenters, and the weavers' workshop.

tomb. It was discovered in the 1920s, and here we have a real chance to take a first hand look at an intact burial. The entrance had been concealed with chips of the rock, and the door below was blocked with a brick wall. The small burial chamber was undecorated, but the coffin and its contents remained in immaculate condition. The body looked like a huge cylinder wrapped in sheets and pads held in place by bandages, with a red shawl tied like a kilt round the waist. The face and upper body of the mummy was covered with a gilt stucco mask showing Waḥ as a thin man with whiskers and moustache. More sheets and pads with a layer of resin appeared underneath, eventually revealing four bead necklaces and a spectacular row of eleven hollow spheroid silver beads.

A string of blue beads and four scarabs of silver and lapis lazuli had been placed on his chest. Under more bandages splashed with resin funerary jewellery had been placed about his body. Altogether 845 square metres of linen had been used for his wrappings, most of it old household linen, but it reveals just how important an industry weaving and spinning must have been.

Waḥ must have relied on provisions from his master, for apart from a meal of bread, beer and meat placed beside his coffin, there was nothing in the tomb to help him along.

The last vizier of the Eleventh dynasty became the first king of the Twelfth. Amenemḥēt was his name, meaning 'Amūn is in front', and in front the god was to be for a good many years. Amūn became the god of the empire, and whoever served this principal national god was guaranteed a brilliant future. The capital and the royal cemetery were shifted to the north to a site called Lisht where the Delta met Upper Egypt. But Thebes became more and more prominent as the home of Amūn and the religious capital. This is reflected in a curious fashion on the tombs of the private individuals. Only one person of the Twelfth dynasty had a spectacular tomb at Thebes, but this was enough to keep the tradition alive and carry it into the New Kingdom, when Thebes was to become the most important burial ground ever in Egypt. Many officials of the period were buried in more modest tombs in the area of Deir el-Baḥri. Before we look at the tomb of Antefoḳer which bridges the gap between the decorated tombs of the Eleventh dynasty and those of the New Kingdom, we may look at one of the many burials of the less well-to-do Thebans in the Twelfth dynasty. It was discovered in December 1823 by J. Passalacqua (see below, p. 104). His description and accompanying drawing are more detailed than was customary for excavators at that time, and the find remains together to this day in the museum in East Berlin. The engraving in Passalacqua's publication gives us a unique glimpse of what was probably an everyday event in those days. Most of his contemporaries would have thrown themselves on the spoils without bothering to take notes. The coffin of a steward named Mentuḥotp is surrounded by two servant statues; two funerary boats; four storage jars with clay stoppers having once contained Nile water; the head and shoulder of a bull; two plates with cakes resting on twigs of sycomore; two wooden sticks; and a neck rest. The find as such is perhaps nothing out of the ordinary. But the drawing of it is.

The mummy was wrapped in linen bandages and pads and had as its only ornaments a fayence necklace, and a figurine showing the deceased was placed on the chest of the body. The mummy itself was in a very fragile condition and disintegrated when the coffins were extricated from the tomb.

In the Twelfth dynasty, when the political centre moved to the north, the capital and the royal burial ground was at Lisht near the oasis of Fayûm. In the reign of Sesostris I, at the very beginning of the dynasty, Antefoḳer, vizier and governor of Thebes, chose to have his tomb near

FIGURE 21
The burial of Mentuḥotp. From the frontispiece of Passalacqua's publication.

the place where he performed his duties. It remains the sole representative of a decorated Twelfth dynasty tomb in this area, and we do not know whether we can call it a typical tomb of the period. It probably was, for it bridges the gap very well between the tombs of the Old and the New Kingdoms. In one respect, though, it is unusual. As mentioned above, decorated tombs for private persons of the female sex are virtually non-existent. Women are present in the tombs as mothers, wives or daughters, never in their own right, and never take precedence over their husbands. In Antefoḳer's tomb (no. 60) the situation is different. Not only does a lady called Senet appear more frequently, and also on her own on the walls, but in some cases the texts are written exclusively for her. Though now known as the tomb of Antefoḳer, it would be more correct to call it 'the tomb of the lady Senet'. The reason for this state of affairs has not been satisfactorily explained, nor has the fact that the figure of Antefoḳer has been mutilated in many of the scenes. At some stage the tomb was burnt out, causing a distortion of the colours and leaving the plaster in a very fragile condition where the straw in the

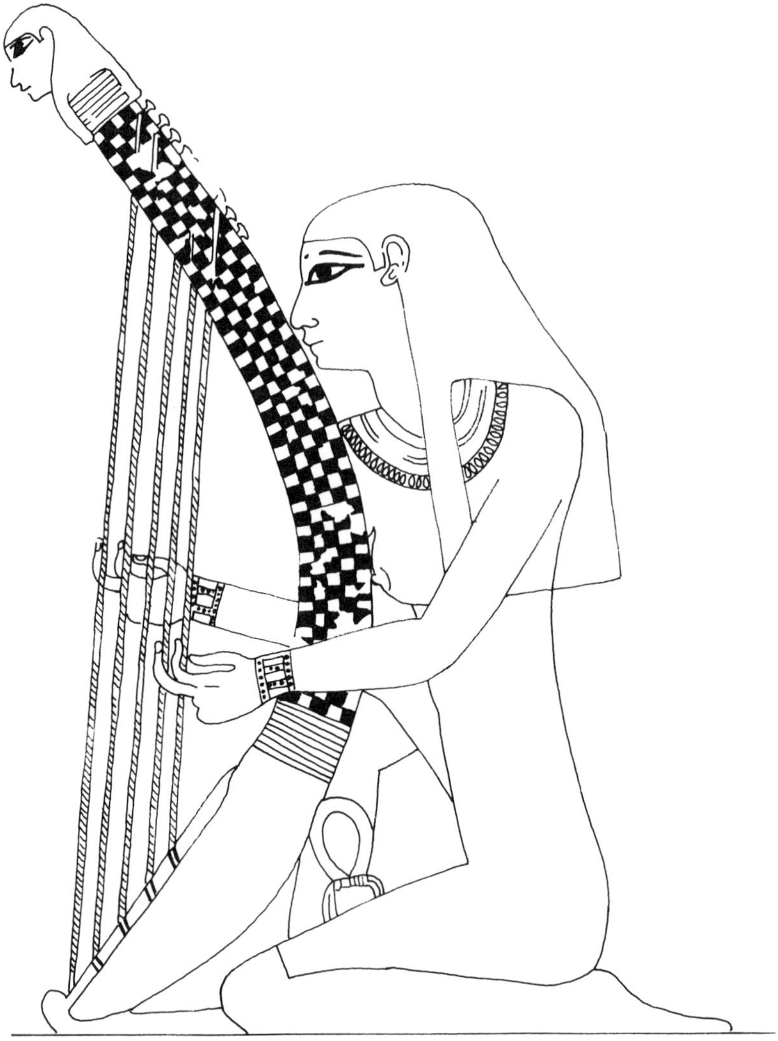

FIGURE 22
Lady playing a harp in TT 60.

mud was burnt away. Nevertheless, thanks to N. de G. Davies, who published the tomb (see below) we are able to obtain a very good impression of the tomb and its decoration.

Like the tomb of Nofru at Deir el-Baḥri, this one was a point of pilgrimage and sightseeing. Visitors came here at the beginning of the Eighteenth dynasty, and those among them who could write (mainly scribes) left a record of the visit on the walls. One is of particular interest, for it was scribbled by Amenemḥēt, a scribe, counter of grain and steward of the vizier of Tuthmosis III. He later decorated his own tomb (no. 82) in the neighbourhood and somehow got his artist to copy some of the scenes for his own tomb.

Antefoḳer's tomb (no. 60) probably provided the inspiration for later tombs of the Eighteenth dynasty in many respects. It consists of a long corridor sunk straight into the mountain side, but the later so typical transverse hall is lacking. The shaft descends from the rear end of the corridor. The scenes of the funeral procession, combined with the representation of the voyage to Abydos, are to be found on the left wall; the hunting and fishing and fowling are on the right wall, as was common in the Eighteenth dynasty; and a figure of the tomb owner and his wife greet the visitors at the rear end of the tomb.

Among the subjects we find many which are the immediate predecessors of those in the later tombs, both in content and execution. A basic activity like work in the fields never changed much, but all the individual phases are present and are rendered in the same way: ploughing and sowing; harvesting the grain with a sickle and leaving the straw on the ground; a man with his sickle tucked under his arm and drinking from a water jar; provisions laid out in the shade of a tree; carrying the corn in a hemispherical basket to the threshing ground; threshing with oxen and winnowing by girls who protect their hair with a scarf and use scoops for throwing the grain into the air; recording the grain and storing it in granaries. The harvesting of grapes is also included, but it is rendered with fewer details, and the pressing of the grapes is not shown. Activities in the kitchen inspired the artist to draw baking, brewing, roasting fowl and threading meat onto strings in a fashion which was so vividly displayed in the models of Meketrēʿ.

Hunting in the desert is nearly indistinguishable from later scenes, showing the tomb owner striding in the desert accompanied by his servant and shooting his arrows at the beasts which have been trapped in a stockade on the pink sand. It is interesting to find the fishing and fowling here in its final form. In the Old Kingdom tomb of Kheti it had merely been suggested. The full significance of the scene will be explained below. In Antefoḳer's tomb we have the symmetrical representation of the tomb owner in two canoes on either side of a papyrus thicket. Unfortunately the scene is too damaged to distinguish many details.

The voyage to Abydos and the funeral ceremonies are naturally archaising and continued to be so in the New Kingdom, and no development can be expected here. The banquet scene, which has such prominence later, is here more rudimentary and without the significant little details which later reveal its *raison d'être*. But one of the central pictures in the tomb suggests that the underlying ideas may have been the same. Senet is being presented with food offerings, a bowl of unguent and a mirror – three basic requirements for survival which appear in tombs as early as the Predynastic period.

The Middle Kingdom was followed by a second 'intermediate period', when Egypt was in the hands of foreigners for some one hundred years. No decorated tombs of any consequence appear to have survived from these years, but burials, notably on the lower slopes of the hills at Draʿ Abû el-Nagaʿ have yielded many interesting smaller objects such as toilet equipment, furniture, figurines, musical instruments as well as the coffins in which the Thebans of the time were buried. Where the coffins had previously been rectangular they now tend to adopt the shape of the human figure. The surface was decorated with a pattern of feathers and, along the sides, scenes of funerary nature: offerings, slaughter, funeral procession and so on, in short subjects which, if the owner were in more fortunate circumstances, would have been depicted on the walls of a more expensive tomb chapel.

3
THE EIGHTEENTH DYNASTY
(1575–1335 BC)

The Theban tombs of the Eighteenth dynasty have a uniform character which sets them apart from tombs from other periods and sites. The architectural features may vary though the basic requirements remain the same for most tombs of this period. At Thebes one particular type of tomb is more frequent than any other, and the so-called T-shaped tomb is the one that has set the standard.

FIGURE 23
Plan of a T-shaped tomb: TT 77.

As far as the decoration of the rooms is concerned it remains an inexplicable fact that with very few exceptions the only site of New Kingdom date in Egypt which has tombs with painted decoration is the Theban necropolis. The tombs elsewhere are sculpted. The absence of painted tombs of this date at other sites cannot be due to the nature of the rock where tombs were traditionally cut, for painted tombs of the period before and after the New Kingdom abound all over the country.

Few paintings have survived from monuments other than tombs, and the scenes depicted on the walls of houses, palaces and temples were usually of a different nature. It is therefore a fairly straightforward matter to attribute a picture of a painted tomb, or even a fragment of a tomb painting, of a suitable date to the Theban necropolis. A representation in relief is more difficult to place. We have already had occasion to mention Wensu's tomb (no. A4) which is so similar to the tomb of Paḥeri at el-Kâb. If Paḥeri's tomb had disappeared, and we were left with just a handful of copies of the scenes drawn by the early travellers, for example, and no provenance for them, it would be very difficult to place these scenes elsewhere but at Thebes. Usually minor differences in style will reveal the hand of a provincial artist. The case of Wensu and Paḥeri is atypical, but perhaps less so than we realise. In Egypt, where so much is lost, an exception may be closer to the rule than the evidence suggests.

The T-shaped tomb is the only outstanding architectural form of any consistency in the Eighteenth dynasty. Ideally such a tomb should comprise the following elements: (1) a forecourt, partly cut in the rock, partly built of mud brick, with a gate; (2) upper rock-cut chambers including (a) a transverse hall; (b) an elongated passage; (c) an inner room with a niche for statues or rock-cut statues at the rear wall; (3) a shaft and subterranean burial chamber, inaccessible after the burial. The position of many tombs high up on the hill side prevented large courts being laid out but usually some sort of arrangement provided an attractive entrance to the tomb. Funerary cones (cf. above, p. 15) made a decorative frieze above the doorway, and, if space permitted, the tomb was crowned by a little pyramid.

The number of subjects depicted on the walls of the tomb is limited, but a skilful artist would know how to exert his talents within the given framework. Many of the scenes can be enjoyed for the sheer beauty of the colour and the elegance of their lines and composition. But only when one is able to read the message conveyed by the ancient artists can their skill and ingenuity be fully appreciated. Hieroglyphs are pictures; pictures are letters; and all pictures have a magic quality. The representations on the walls become alive and can be beneficial or harmful. They had to be chosen with the utmost care, and they had to be absolutely correct to function in the way in which they were intended. Woe betide the tomb owner whose decoration was interfered with!

The preoccupation of the Egyptian with rebirth can be read on every single wall of his tomb. At any rate the Egyptians themselves could read it, and we are beginning to understand what it is all about. We have been able to read the hieroglyphs for the past one hundred and fifty years, but the code of the *pictures* has only recently been deciphered. The more we look around, the more evident it is that we are on the right track. Strangely it was not the funerary scenes which were difficult to interpret, but the 'scenes of daily life'. The generally accepted interpretation that they were indeed scenes of daily life projected into eternity was not entirely satisfactory. They were far too idealised to present a true picture of the way in which the inhabitants of Thebes could be expected to behave. Who would go fowling in festive outfit in a minute canoe with wife and children, and who would go hunting for a hippopotamus when the beast had long since disappeared from the area? Did not the guests ever have anything to eat at those banquets? When it comes to detail in the representations one must often ask 'why here?'. Once a few of these questions had found an answer the path was paved for the rest, and perhaps we can now begin to grasp some hidden aspects of funerary beliefs and practices.

These remarks apply to many, though not all 'scenes of daily life'. The tomb was also a monument to the deceased, a medium by means of which he was able to immortalise the most important part of his life: his work in the service of the king. All scenes in the tomb had a part to play, supplementing one another in projecting the tomb owner's personality and enabling him to continue his existence beyond the grave.

By any standards the king was the most important person in the life of a tomb owner, and for this reason he was the largest figure on the walls of the tomb. In the Eighteenth dynasty at Thebes it was apparently

FIGURE 24
King Amenophis III (TT 57).

not considered preposterous to include pictures of the sovereign among those of ordinary mortals, though some tomb owners, whose office did not involve daily contact with his person, chose to omit such a scene. Representations of the king are very rarely found in private tombs at other sites. Usually the king was given the most prominent wall-space available, being shown on either side of the doorway leading from the transverse hall to the inner rooms of the tomb, frequently in a symmetrical representation, seated with his back to the doorway. Thus he caught the blaze of light from outside and was never overlooked. He is seated in his full regalia under a canopy. Facing him, outside the shelter, the tomb owner may be shown paying his respects.

A scene showing the office of the tomb owner is linked to the representation of the king if there is an obvious connection between the two. The vizier, the high priests of Amūn, and army personnel were in direct contact with the king in real life, and their functions inspired the artists to masterly depictions within the limits agreed upon.

FIGURE 25
The official representation of the tomb owner (TT 79).

FIGURE 27
Crafts to be supervised by the tomb owner: makers of chariots and archery equipment, and metal workers (TT 66).

The duties of the vizier and certain other officials included receiving tribute on behalf of the sovereign. Foreigners from all corners of the empire came to Egypt with their merchandise: bearded yellow-skinned Syrians with costly vases; curly-haired Cretans bearing strange receptacles; black Nubians with rings of gold; equally dark-skinned people from Africa bringing myrrh, incense and exotic animals. All these goods were recorded and transferred to the temple or the palace.

Supervision of workshops came within the duties of the vizier or, for the temple workshops, the high priests of Amūn. Carpenters, metalworkers, potters, brickmakers, leatherworkers, chariotmakers and jewellers work busily under the gaze of their master with no end to their task in sight. Only rarely did the craftsmen themselves have the means to procure a tomb on the walls of which they could display their occupation as their own.

Military men, governors or mayors would depict scenes of the life of the soldier in their tombs. As the owner was the person in charge

FIGURE 26
The official representation of the tomb owner's wife in her capacity as chief royal nurse (TT 85).

of the operations, he would show how he lined up his men, fed and clothed them, and marched them along in procession accompanied by trumpets and drums.

Officials of the granary chose to depict the operations of measuring the fields, transporting the grain and recording it in the granary or celebrating a harvest festival. Like many others they probably already had agricultural scenes on the tomb walls, but those served a different (or at least dual) purpose, as we shall see below. The same applies to representations of cows and bulls. Any large estate would have cattle, but it is only in the tomb of an overseer of cattle that the detailed representation of the stables would find a place.

Some professions were obviously more suitable for depiction than others. In the tomb of a 'chief servant who weighs the silver and gold of the estate of Amūn' the weighing of metal was easy to represent; and the 'overseer of works on the two great obelisks in the temple of Amūn' had no trouble in explaining that he wanted the manufacture of the obelisks in question shown in his tomb. The 'harbour master of the Southern City (Thebes)' shows the inspection of ships with foreign produce; the physician commemorates the occasion when a foreign nobleman consulted him; and the butlers are shown overseeing the wine in their charge. Perhaps it would be more difficult to visualise what a 'head of the secrets in the chest of Anubis' would be doing during his working hours.

These scenes are most frequently to be found in the transverse hall of a T-shaped tomb, or in a part of the tomb near the entrance. On either side of the entrance doorway, and thus frequently just opposite the representation of the king, the tomb owner is shown offering on braziers and/or libating to gods who are not depicted, but who are mentioned in the accompanying text. The tomb owner takes up almost the full length of the wall, but because the king on the opposite side is seated, the tomb owner remains at a scale which does not exceed the figure of the sovereign. He faces the entrance, lifting up his offerings to Amūn-Reʿ, Rēʿ-Ḥarakhti or Osiris-Wennūfer. Sometimes the libating is omitted, and the scene loses its symmetry. A sub-scene with offering-bringers and butchers is often inserted below. By the middle of the Eighteenth dynasty the tomb owner's wife, or rarely his mother, joins him in the ritual, which is actually part of the Feast of the Valley to be described below.

The fishing and fowling scene is strictly symmetrical, one never occurring without the other. In the centre grows a clump of papyrus where the artist, if he was imaginative, took the opportunity of depicting birds and insects. On either side rests a small canoe with the tomb owner standing upright, frozen in the act of spearing his two fish or hitting a bird with a throwstick. Members of his family are on board or standing by. The river, shown almost as if in section, reveals a myriad of fishes, birds and, less agreeably, a crocodile.

The key to a proper understanding of this scene lies in the two fish

No. 365. Part 1. Fowling scene. Part 2. Spearing fish with the bident. *The*

1. An amateur sportsman throwing the stick.
2. His son, holding a fresh stick ready, and carrying the game.
3, 4. His daughters or sisters. 5. Another son, carrying the game.
6. A decoy bird, with its nest in the boat.
7. An ichneumon, carrying away a young bird from a nest.
8. Two bulti fish speared with the bident of *fig.* 11.
9, 10. Butterflies and dragon-flies.
12. His sister, holding a spear.
13. His son, holding a spear, and carrying the fish strung upon a water-plant. The cat appears as if begging to be let out of the boat into the thicket.

The same person is represented, and the hieroglyphic inscriptions record the action of fishing and fowling and his name, Mutsa, third priest of Amen, superintend of the treasury, who is accompanied by his sister Bati, a virgin of Amen, and his son User ha.

FIGURE 28
Fishing and fowling (TT A24). From Wilkinson, *Manners and Customs* (ed. Birch), ii.107 (No. 365).

which are right in the centre, with the harpoon pointing straight at them as if the artist is willing us to see them. The fish are *tilapia* which have the habit of swallowing their young when in danger, but expectorating them unharmed once the crisis is over. This curious habit had not escaped the attention of the Egyptians. The way they saw it the little ones had died, but had been miraculously reborn. This coincided with their own hopes, and the *tilapia* thus became a symbol of rebirth. The whole picture is built around this idea, with details lifted from the banquet scenes. Fowling was woven into the scene presenting another aspect of the idea of rebirth: being able to go fowling in the Hereafter was a visible sign of strength and ability to function. Osiris himself, when departing from the world of the living, not only had speech and movement restored to him but most specifically his ability to go fowling.

The tomb owner's canoe sometimes carries an unusual passenger: a duck or goose standing in the prow of the boat, or once in a while a duckling is cradled in the palm of the tomb owner's daughter. A charming detail, but since we are concerned with the art of Egypt, this is not solely a decorative element. Whenever a duck is shown, the context is usually tinged with eroticism. The Egyptians knew about the beginning of life, and although they had no way of grasping the mystery to the full, they knew that contact between a man and a woman could cause a new being. The preliminaries were part of the process, and anything to do with them must not be neglected, particularly if it was one's own rebirth which was being prepared. The duck was an erotic symbol, and the bird was discreetly introduced into what was nearly its natural habitat in order to assist the tomb owner on the path to eternal life.

Fishing and fowling is shown either in the hall of the tomb or on one of the walls of the passage where its elongated shape suited the format of the wall.

Spearing a hippopotamus was included in the scene in the first half of the dynasty, but it was a separate representation requiring a third figure of the tomb owner. Aesthetically it was not a satisfactory solution although the individual scenes with the hippo are done with artistry reminiscent of older representations of the same subject.

With hunting in the desert the scene changes to firmer ground: pink speckled sand. The tomb owner is out hunting either on foot or in his chariot, accompanied by his servants (or in one instance by his wife).

FIGURE 29
Detail of a hunting scene (TT 276).

The Egyptians were never great landscape painters. The scenery is suggested by the undulating dunes of sand and a few items of vegetation. But the animals living there are beautifully captured in their flying gallop or sleeping under a shrub. The arrows of the tomb owner make the scenery less idyllic. The servants carrying back the trophies of the hunt show that the hunter means business.

It is difficult to gauge the significance of this scene. The desert was a mighty enemy; its red colour was the colour of Seth, 'god of confusion'; and to conquer its inhabitants was in a manner of speaking to avert all evil in advance.

Although the subject was admirably suited to a tall, narrow wall, such as the end walls of the transverse hall, where it was sometimes placed, the part of the tomb most frequently chosen was the right wall of the passage, nearest to the entrance, sharing the wall with funerary rites. It is perhaps significant that the subject was particularly favoured during the reign of Tuthmosis III, one of the two great 'sporting pharaohs'.

In an agricultural society like Egypt most of our tomb owners would have been able to cultivate a patch of land in order to be self-sufficient with the basic requirements. In this way agricultural representations in

FIGURE 30
Scribes leading cows to be counted (TT 57)

the tombs may be said to be autobiographical. We are shown how the soil was tilled, seeds are sown, and the grain is harvested by cutting the ears and leaving the stubble in the field; the ears are taken to the threshing ground, worked by oxen, winnowed by farmhands and eventually measured in bushels and recorded. Needless to say the tomb owner is never doing the hard work himself. He sits comfortably in the shade of an arbour engaged in the favourite Egyptian pastime: inspecting someone else's work.

Agriculture was the very backbone of life in Egypt. All other activities revolved around it. Grain was everything: food and money, and at the best of times the granaries were spilling over. No wonder that any Egyptian, be he a land owner or not, would want this basic activity depicted on the walls of his tomb. If the relatives ceased to bring food offerings; if the priests failed to recite the offering formulas; if perhaps the offering tables depicted in the tomb ran out of supplies; if these disasters took place it was good to know that the little men on the walls would soon produce another crop, and all would be right again.

Scenes of vintage presumably served a similar purpose in providing the tomb owner with fresh and constant supplies in the Hereafter. The grapes are picked and pressed and the wine bottled, and the jars stacked in the cellars. A butler, a steward, or a temple official in charge of the wine cellar of the temple would choose this subject as a matter of course, but it occurs in far more tombs than the number of vineyards in Thebes would justify, and it has obviously become a conventional representation. It is usually positioned in the right part of the tomb, preferably in the hall, and it is very often a sub-scene to fishing and fowling.

Of all the traditional scenes in the Theban tombs the funeral proces-

FIGURE 31
The grape gatherer (TT 261).

FIGURE 32
The coffin being dragged to the necropolis (TT 54).

sion was one which was never omitted. The procession would be heading for the inner rooms of the tomb, and therefore it is usually represented on the walls as walking in this direction, almost invariably on the left wall of the elongated passage of a T-shaped tomb, or on the corresponding wall of a tomb of a different shape. Most figures in funerary processions therefore face to the right.

The subject itself is very complex when represented in full, but all the details do not necessarily correspond to events which actually took place at a funeral in the Eighteenth dynasty. The episodes appear to be copied from representations of the Middle Kingdom, which were in turn based on ideas of Old Kingdom date. The procession to the embalming house and the dragging of the coffin to the tomb were of course unchanged, and so was the scene in front of the tomb with the mourners, the grieving widow embracing her husband's mummy or coffin (the opposite is never shown!) and the ablutions and fumigations before the coffin was lowered into the bowels of the earth.

The voyage to Abydos is perhaps the most obviously symbolic representation in the tomb. In theory everyone wished to travel to Abydos and pay their respects to Osiris, King of the Dead, at his traditional burial place. This may have happened to some in real life, but in the tombs the scenes are stylised and not of this world. A boat with the deceased couple (a wife is always included) followed by another with a coffin completely enshrouded in a patterned cloth drift downstream to Abydos and, in a continuous representation, sail upstream with sails unfurled and with its mission completed.

FIGURE 33
A sailor on board a boat heading for Abydos (TT 139).

The scene is often, though not always, placed in connection with the funeral procession, either as a sub-scene or in a register of the same height. The symbolic significance of the representation is emphasised in the rites performed during one of the annual festivals in the necropolis, when model boats were placed in the tomb to help the deceased undertake his journey. At midnight the boats were turned round so that he could travel home again.

The Opening of the Mouth was performed on the dead person's mummy or a statue of him in order to enable him to speak and eat again. A whole series of episodes makes up the complete ritual, but an abbreviated version was often considered adequate. The subject is particularly elaborately rendered during the first half of the Eighteenth dynasty, but on the other hand it is not compulsory. It is very frequently symmetrically arranged with scenes from the funeral procession on the opposite wall of the passage, but there are many exceptions to this. As a general rule the mummy or statue faces the entrance of the tomb with the mortuary priests looking in the opposite direction.

One of the most attractive subjects in the tombs is the banquet scenes where Thebans of the upper middle class of 3500 years ago are shown at their ease, smiling, drinking, gazing at one another with big dark eyes and listening to music and song. We do not require any explanations to enjoy these scenes, where the artist was able to introduce the latest fashion into an otherwise conventional representation. Hair styles are a reliable criterion of dating in any sophisticated civilisation, and so also in Egypt. Each reign had its own characteristics captured by the clever

FIGURE 34
Arranging the curls of the wig for the banquet (TT 38).

artist, who added other details like jewellery and floral diadems to give a contemporary touch to his picture.

However charming the banquet scene is as an ideal picture of a happy occasion, it must also have fulfilled a function in the scheme of decoration as a whole. It is the little details which reveal the *raison d'être* of the subject, and they all point in the same direction. We are dealing here with the preliminaries to creating a new being, the deceased reborn, the symbolism being borrowed from the language of daily life.

Take the lotus flower, for example. The men and women in the picture carry it in their hands, the flowers adorn their necks and the wigs of the ladies. The lotus was a symbol of rebirth: according to one legend the sun god himself was born out of a lotus flower. The mandrake fruit carried the same connotations at a different level. The women play games with the fruit, hiding it behind their backs and sniffing it. It was poisonous, so it was not part of the evening's fare. It was a sign that Eros was among them, as if we had not guessed already from the way

FIGURE 35
A lady at a banquet.
Fragment of wall-painting from the tomb of Nebamūn now in the British Museum.

they are dressed up: semi-transparent robes, revealing more than concealing, and on top the pride of any Egyptian lady: her wig, used for special occasions. In all societies hair is closely related to sexuality; any dramatic change in fashion, like the long haired youths of the 1960s, is felt as 'weird' because it interferes with the borders we have set between the sexes. In Egyptian representations the importance of hair was emphasised in substituting a heavy and elaborately curled wig. Wigs were worn in bed. 'Don your wig and let us spend a happy hour!' says the amorous young man in a tale.

FIGURE 36
Preparing the bed and a chair, and bringing in supplies of unguent and eye paint for the union of the couple (TT 260).

Sometimes this subject has an additional vignette on another wall: the bed is actually being prepared, with mirror and eye paint close to hand underneath the bed. The wig was crowned by an unguent cone, a lump of scented fat which was remodelled during the course of the evening as the fat melted and enveloped the wig and clothes in fragrant grease. Scent played an important part in the erotic imagination of the Egyptians. 'Your scent is like someone from incense land,' says one lover in a poem. 'Your fragrance is all over me,' cries another.

Although husband and wife as tomb owners are seated next to each other, tenderly embracing, the same privilege is usually not accorded to the guests at the banquet. There is a women's corner and a men's corner, although there is nothing to suggest that they are not in the same room or courtyard. As the girls cannot embrace their husbands they embrace one another, lifting up a curl of the neighbour's wig, grasping her wrist, holding a hand poised over her lap, or playing with mandrake fruits. The servants, naked boys or girls, see to their needs. Food is not served, but no one lacks for a drink. Some have had one too many and relieve themselves by being sick in a corner. The servants keep pouring wine and beer, flavoured with date juice to taste. The Egyptians would know what this act of pouring really meant, for they were very fond of plays on words. The word to pour consisted of the same letters as the word used to describe a sexual act. The entire banquet scene had one definite purpose, rendered in the discreetest of terms: to hint again and again at the proper atmosphere for creating new life.

The banquet was often depicted in close proximity to the scene showing episodes from the Feast of the Valley, the annual summer celebrations in the necropolis when a statue of Amūn was made to travel from its shrine at Karnak across the river. The god was accompanied by a host of priests, priestesses and musicians. The statue was carried up and down the winding paths among the tombs to greet the deceased and their relatives who had come to see the god. The tomb owner himself

FIGURE 37
The bouquet of Amūn being presented to the tomb owner and his wife on the occasion of the Feast of the Valley (TT 161).

was visualised as offering to the gods as they passed the doorway of the tomb, lifting up braziers with bread, fowl and incense and pouring myrrh in the god's path. A special bouquet of Amūn consisting of papyrus stems, lotus flowers, mandrake and poppy was placed in the tomb for the deceased to enjoy. The priestesses shook their sistra and rattled their necklaces as they passed, and special festive offerings were instituted. It was an occasion of joy and happiness to everyone.

These are some of the most characteristic subjects to be found on the walls of the tombs of the Eighteenth dynasty. Scenes of offering are very common, too, but they are to be taken at their face value and are a mere precaution to ensure a continuous supply of sustenance. This was epitomised at the focal point of the tomb, the rear wall of the inner room, where a statue of the deceased presided as recipient of it all.

The tombs of the Eighteenth dynasty are scattered all over the necropolis from Deir el-Medîna in the south to Dra' Abû el-Naga' in the north, but some sites were in particular demand.

The tombs at Deir el-Medîna are a special case, in that the site was chosen only by members of the local community: people who were in some way connected with work on the tombs of the royal family. By the reign of Tuthmosis IV the community was firmly established, though judging from the surviving evidence it reached its maximum activity under the Ramessid kings. Six decorated tombs of Eighteenth dynasty

date have been identified, the most significant of these being that of Khaᶜ, the architect (no. 8), not only because of its decorated upper chamber of modest proportions, but especially due to the fact that the burial chamber below was found intact, containing all the items which had been placed there some 3300 years earlier: furniture, boxes and baskets full of interesting items from daily life, garments, wigs, unguents and a vast array of food, herbs and spices which makes the find particularly valuable for scholars with an interest in these necessities. It is, for instance, fascinating that one of the pots in the tomb contained an opium unguent which had a fatal effect when injected into a frog!

The little hill which conceals Deir el-Medîna from view from the valley, called Qurnet Muraᶜi, also has six tombs of the Eighteenth dynasty. One (no. 40) is of particular interest, for it once sheltered the mummy of Ḥuy, viceroy of Nubia in the reign of Tutᶜankhamūn. The paintings on the walls of the upper chamber, though applied on a coarse surface of mud mixed with straw and hardly any grounding, reflect the characteristics of the art of the late Amarna period, well known from the artefacts from the tomb of Tutᶜankhamūn himself. We recognise the large heads of the figures with prominent eyes and lips, the rounded chins and supple limbs. One of the walls of the tomb shows Ḥuy in his office receiving tribute from Nubia on behalf of his king, introducing new details into a conventional representation such as a Nubian princess being led before

FIGURE 39
Tribute bearers bringing goods from Syria (TT 40). From Hay MSS 29851, 369–86.

FIGURE 38
Objects from the tomb of Khaʿ and his wife Meryt. Courtesy Museo Egizio, Turin.

the king in a vehicle drawn by oxen, sheltered from the blazing sun by a large fan, depicted in such a lively fashion that we can almost hear the lowing of the beasts and the hustle and bustle of the procession, and smell the odour of the giraffes, the baboons and the bearers.

Ḥuy's colleague and perhaps immediate predecessor had been buried next door. The decorated chamber of Merymosi's tomb (no. 383) has long since been burnt out, leaving just traces of hieroglyphs on the walls. When it was rediscovered some fifty years ago, a local family had settled down in its once splendid pillared hall, and the adjoining rooms were used as stables. But the funerary cones, which were once inset as a frieze along the upper edge of the façade of the tomb, have survived in great number, eighty-five being found by the excavators alone. A door jamb was found lying in the tomb of Ḥuy, and three stelae from the tomb were likewise recovered. Most interesting perhaps are Merymosi's coffins. He had no less than three sarcophagi of stone, and probably more coffins of wood inside, one inserted in the other. The lid of the intermediate sarcophagus is now in the collections of the British Museum along with some other fragments. All three were shaped like a mummy and were decorated with representations of funerary deities which would protect Merymosi on his journey in the Hereafter. To little avail, for Merymosi has long since become dust.

Almost a hundred years earlier the overseer of the treasury had chosen the same attractive site for his house for eternity. Amenemōpet's tomb (no. 276) has achieved less fame than that of Ḥuy and virtually no publication. Its walls suffered from tomb robberies during World War II, but still enough survives to give an impression of the craftsmanship of the ancient artist. As treasurer Amenemōpet depicted himself receiving solid rings of gold brought from Nubia and also showed how the precious metal was transformed to vases and jewellery in the workshops. The conventional scene of hunting in the desert shows the artist carrying out his brief in a very decent fashion, though perhaps not with the artistry displayed in other tombs.

There can be no doubt that the most popular burial place at Thebes was at Sheikh ʿAbd el-Qurna. More than half the tombs of the necropolis of the dynasty are crowded together on the slopes of this hill, making a total of no fewer than one hundred and ten Eighteenth dynasty tombs at this site alone. Tomb after tomb perforated the hillside like a honeycomb, being so close together that an earlier tomb was often accidentally met with by the stonemasons chipping away at the cliff. The tombs in the plain below are slightly more spaced out, though the next tomb is always within reach.

It is at Sheikh ʿAbd el-Qurna that we find the tombs of Nakht (no. 52) and Menna (no. 69) so frequently visited by coach loads of tourists that the authorities decided to keep the doors locked for the time being to give the wall paintings a rest from the humid breath and flash lights of the visitors. But there are other splendid tombs to see. Userḥēt (tomb

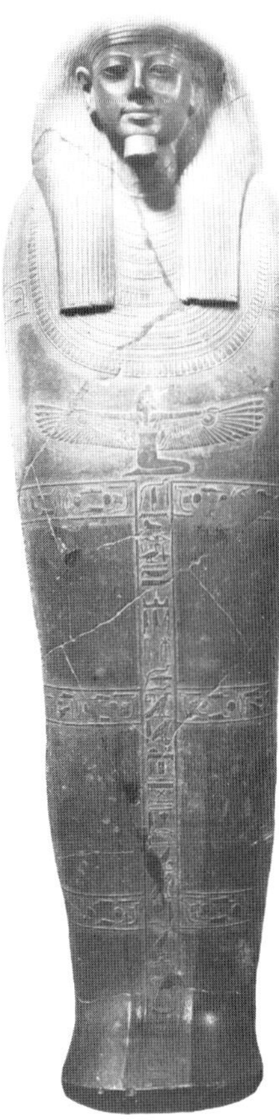

FIGURE 40
The coffin of Merymosi now in the British Museum.

FIGURE 41
Soldiers lining up to have their heads shaven (TT 56).

no. 56) was a scribe who obviously coped with the logistics of the army of Amenophis II. He shows how the soldiers were lined up for their meal, how the barbers came to shave them and how neat the final result was. The hunting scene in this tomb is particularly successful with interesting details such as a fox being caught hanging in a tree.

The tomb of Khaʿemḥēt (no. 57) may be disappointing at first sight, for it is almost entirely deprived of colour. But the delicacy of the limestone relief and the vivacity of the scenes emphasise the skill of the sculptor. Khaʿemḥēt was overseer of the granaries of Upper and Lower Egypt. Perhaps this fact prompted him to have two scenes with agricultural activities sculpted in his tomb, not just the usual one representation. One of them shows the whole range of conventional episodes from ploughing to harvesting, with numerous less common details such as a boy taking a break from his labours to play his pipe, and the climax to the season's efforts: offerings being presented to the god of harvest. This series of events is more familiar to us from the painted tombs of Nakht and Menna. But there is evidence to suggest that the painter and sculptor drew their inspiration from the same sources. In fact, some details from the tomb of Khaʿemḥēt are duplicated in a painted tomb of which only fragments survive. It is not customary for field workers to wear sandals, however practical it may seem to be able to protect one's feet from the stubble in the field. In the two tombs in question the men who jump high in the air to force down the lid of a giant basket of grain certainly have been provided with identical footwear. Other interesting details and parallels with regard to the fragmentary tomb will be discussed below.

We have touched on the question of similarities in tomb decoration above, p. 14–15. Within the area of Sheikh ʿAbd el-Qurna we meet another interesting case: the tombs of Menna (no. 69) and Pairi (no. 139). Menna's tomb is thought to have been decorated just before that of Pairi (only the latter has a date written in it). Certain representations in the two tombs are so similar in their composition that one (Pairi) has been taken to be a pastiche on the other, the painter of the tomb of Pairi showing a less elegant hand and less attractive choice of colours than the artist who worked in the tomb of Menna. Only part of the decoration in the tomb of Pairi survives, but it is unlikely that the tombs should have been identical in their concept as a whole – the Egyptians just did not duplicate tombs to such an extent. But again one is almost forced to conclude that the two painters made use of the same 'pages' of a 'pattern book', so that the general design remained the same for certain scenes, yet the final result reveals the different personalities and skills of two artists.

The lower slope of the hill was chosen by a man whose tomb (no. 55) ended up looking rather different from what he had planned at first. Raʿmosi was the most influential private individual of his time. He was mayor of Thebes and vizier. His career began in the reign of Amenophis III and extended into that of Amenophis IV, and it is precisely this

FIGURE 42
The tomb of Raʿmosi: wall decorated in the conventional style (TT 55).

fact that makes him and his tomb so interesting. Amenophis IV was the 'heretical' king who emphasised the cult of the sun's disc at the expense of all other deities. Not only did the contents of representations change, but the way in which the characters were depicted underwent a transformation which must at the time have been considered even more revolutionary than we are able to grasp today with the millennia separating us from the event.

Raʿmosi had grand ideas for his tomb. The hall was not just to be the upper stroke of the T of a T-shaped tomb. It was turned into a spacious hall with a roof supported by papyriform columns. These have long since fallen, but have been reconstructed in modern times. Raʿmosi decided on the most durable form of tomb decoration: painted relief, and he had chosen the site of his monument in an area where the white limestone was of excellent quality. The decoration on the two walls adjoining the entrance doorway was successfully completed by the sculptors, but the painters seem to have been kept busy elsewhere. On the wall to the left on entering they began to lay out a representation in several registers showing the funeral procession to the tomb, the coffin being dragged along on a sledge, followed by mourning relatives and professional weeping women, as well as by people carrying the numerous items of funerary furniture. The stonemasons were still busy carving their way through the rock to shape the inner chambers of the tomb, while the more delicate operations took place in the hall. But before

FIGURE 43
The tom of Raᶜmosi: detail of wall decorated in 'Amarna' style. Raᶜmosi is shown with prominent lips and jaws, narrow slanting eyes, and a body adapting the contours of a woman's body (TT 55).

the painters were able to complete the decoration of the wall, which would most certainly have had a representation of the voyage to Abydos below the funeral procession, they were told to halt.

The old king had gone to join his forefathers, and his son, Amenophis IV, was in charge as sole ruler and the god's manifestation on earth. The king laid down new principles for representational art. Raᶜmosi had remained in office, but he had to follow suit. Instead of embarking on the costly proceeding of cutting a new tomb he decided to go ahead in the old one, with some modifications. Thus we find the two styles side by side in one and the same tomb, the new decoration being exceedingly similar to that soon to be found in the tombs of el-Amarna, where the king moved with his entourage and officials. Raᶜmosi may have been invited to go, for even before the decoration in the hall had been completed, work was abandoned for good. But this is where we lose track of Raᶜmosi and his family. His tomb remains as a monument of conventional versus controversial concepts of art, a typical example of how nothing old was entirely discarded at the expense of the new in Egypt. But the fact that the tomb remains less completely finished than most indicates that some problems were yet to be overcome in the process.

The adventurous package tourist, who is not put off by having to climb half-way up the hillside among native houses, barking dogs and children posing for photographs with baby goats in their arms, will be rewarded by entering the tomb of Rekhmirēᶜ (no. 100). Rekhmirēᶜ was vizier during the reigns of Tuthmosis III and Amenophis II when things were still as they had always been. No artistic problems had to be overcome in the decoration of his tomb. Yet it ended up showing features different from all other tombs. The tomb is T-shaped as most other tombs of the period. But where all other monuments, tombs and temples alike, become smaller and narrower the further you enter, Rekhmirēᶜ's tomb is just the opposite. The roof of the passage branching off from the transverse entrance hall rises and rises to reach unsurpassed dimensions at the innermost wall of the tomb. This extraordinary phenomenon has not yet found a satisfactory explanation. The scenes depicted on the walls are by no means exceptional, though they are depicted in great detail and with the hand of a master draughtsman. The transverse hall, which has suffered somewhat from the passing of time, has a splendid procession of tribute bringers, it being part of Rekhmirēᶜ's duties as vizier to receive them. Giraffes, baboons, a bear, an elephant and exotic produce are being paraded before our startled gaze. In the passage are shown the workshops in Rekhmirēᶜ's charge: the brickmakers, leatherworkers, metalworkers, sculptors, and jewellers compete with people filling the granaries and storehouses of the king and bakers preparing loaves, cakes and sweetmeats, with hieroglyphs which practically give recipes for us to copy. On the opposite wall the banquet with all its symbolic details is depicted in unusually delicate colours. The funerary rites further in on the walls are among the most elaborate in the necropolis and set the standard for representations of that subject, and of our interpretation

FIGURE 44
A herd of cows (TT 100).

of them. Rekhmirēʿ's statue plays the main part in the ceremonies, replacing the mummy of the great man himself. His eyes are opened to enable him to see again; his mouth is opened to allow him to speak and eat; his bones are made firm in his body, and he is purified with water and incense, while the ancient ritual goes on around him to ensure his resurrection at the other side of the door which led from the innermost chamber to the unknown existence beyond.

A few paces away from Rekhmirēʿ's tomb and possibly still accessible for the dedicated visitor is the tomb of Sennūfer (no. 96). The upper chambers of this tomb are closed to the general public. Behind the massive metal door are stored a great many objects found elsewhere in the

FIGURE 45
Objects from the tomb of Tutʿankhamūn stored in the upper chambers of TT 96.

area, including a number of plain black wooden boxes found in the tomb of Tutʿankhamūn, which are not of interest as works of art and therefore not displayed in the museums of Cairo and Luxor. The wall-paintings of Sennūfer remain, but they are in a state of decay and are not of general interest. But Sennūfer, who was mayor of Thebes in the reign of Amenophis II, had had an unusual idea for his tomb. Usually the burial chambers below are not decorated. But in this case the tomb owner decided to do better than most of his predecessors, and the painters were set to work deep below the surface of the rock, entering from a shaft cut in the forecourt of the tomb. The stonemasons seem to have had problems when trying to smooth the roof of the burial chamber, but an ingenious solution was found to overcome this problem. The person in charge decided to use the bulging ceiling to his advantage, and instead of a geometrical pattern like most other tombs had, a decoration of grapes and vineleaves was decided upon, for which the uneven surface provided the ideal basis. The scenes on the walls, although executed in bold lines and colours and being remarkably well preserved to this day, only serve as the backdrop to this spectacular, undulating ceiling.

The path in front of the tomb continues upwards until one reaches lines of tombs along the upper edge of the hill, descending again on the northern slope. These tombs, being perched on the almost vertical surface of the rock, had little room for forecourts, but had it not been for the interference of man, the rock-cut chambers would have survived even better than they did. Most are roomy tombs with the now familiar transverse hall and elongated passage. Up here we find a few more mayors, viziers and granary officials, but also commanders of soldiers, stewards, prophets of Amūn, overseers of works and fan-bearers of the king. The variety of occupations is reflected in the decoration of the tombs, especially in the walls dedicated to the office of the tomb owner and his particular relation to his king. Those connected with the army or with troups of men recruited to do work in the temples chose to represent these groups of persons of which they were in charge. The artists cleverly decided to represent them with different skin complexions to make the picture interesting, so every other person in the group is shown with a delicate pink skin alternating with men of the conventional dark red.

Amenemḥab, lieutenant-commander of soldiers, was ambitious when talking over the plans for his tomb (no. 85) with his architect. The inner part of the tomb was T-shaped, but in front of the transverse hall another spacious hall was laid out, carved around four square pillars to support the roof, although this device was hardly necessary. The pillars provided extra wallspace in the shape of long panels, a feature known from contemporary royal tombs as well as from some tombs of private individuals. Amenemḥab used two of the faces of the pillars to inscribe hymns to the two kings he had served, Tuthmosis III and Amenophis II, pictures of his wife with a young prince on her lap, whom she had nursed, as well as various scenes of offerings. But perhaps the inner face of the lintel uniting the two central pillars is the most unusual feature of the

FIGURE 46
An artist at work in the tomb of Sennūfer, showing part of the grape ceiling (TT 96).

FIGURE 47
A rare example of 'landscape painting' in Egypt: the tomb owner fighting a hyena (TT 85). Courtesy of the Metropolitan Museum of Art. Photograph by Egyptian Expedition of The Metropolitan Museum of Art.

tomb. The Egyptian painters rarely dealt with 'scenery'. The representations showing 'hunting in the desert' and riverscapes appear to have been the only examples of this genre, the landscape merely suggesting the setting of the activities and not being the main subject at all. Thus they were never forced to tackle the problem of perspective and distance in their works. The painter in charge of Amenemḥab's tomb was not prepared to do this either, but he conceived a unique scene of Amenemḥab fighting a hyena, all alone in a pale desert full of the strangest plants and flowers.

The ʿAsâsîf is the plain which stretches out at the foot of the temple of Deir el-Baḥri. We shall have occasion to explore it in detail when we look at tombs of a later date. Of the two Eighteenth dynasty tombs cut here one is now destroyed, but the other, though partly ruined, is of exceptional interest. The owner, Kharuef, was a contemporary of the vizier Raʿmosi, and his tomb, like that of Raʿmosi, was also decorated with fine reliefs. Kharuef (tomb no. 192) was steward of Queen Teye, spouse of Amenophis III, and this relationship is reflected in the decoration of the tomb. But though Amenophis IV is depicted as king in the tomb, the decoration is executed in the conventional style. A precursor of the spirit of el-Amarna is the emphasis on representations involving the royal family. They are shown offering, going out of the palace, taking part in religious ceremonies and being recipients of offerings, this latter scene being usually the only way for a tomb owner to show his relation to his sovereign.

The little peach-shaped hill of Khôkha is perforated with tombs, about half of which, or thirty-two, are of the Eighteenth dynasty. One of the tombs is particularly well known, not only because the owners were two sculptors in the reign of Amenophis III and because the tomb was well published and the pictures reproduced frequently, but also as a deplorable example of modern vandalism (see below, p. 127). It would have been interesting to find examples of Nebamūn's and Ipuky's skills in their own tomb (no. 181). But the site chosen was ill-suited for the sculpting of reliefs, and the decoration had to be painted on the walls. Whoever was responsible for the work gave to it the best of the artistry of the later half of the dynasty, caught just before the new ideas of Amenophis IV began to manifest themselves. Although the tomb is T-shaped it was cut with surprising disregard for straight lines. In the end the tomb was never finished (did the sculptors go north with the king?). In the hall were depicted the banquet, arts and crafts and the funeral procession. The two colleagues appear together or separately with their families on the walls of the tomb, and it is indeed amazing that few Egyptians thought of this economical way of providing security for life in the Hereafter.

Parennūfer was royal butler 'clean of hands' at the court of Amenophis IV. He followed his master to el-Amarna and had a tomb decorated there. But before the move he had already been busy preparing a tomb at Thebes (no. 188), to which he seems later to have returned for his burial. The tomb is partly in relief, partly in painting and already shows some of the characteristics of the so-called 'Amarna' style although the city after which it was named had hardly been laid out at the time.

One of the most elaborate tombs in the area belonged to Puyemrēʿ, second prophet of Amūn (no. 39). It has a pillared hall, a transverse hall, and no less than three chapels at the rear, the focal points of which showed (1) the tomb owner kneeling before Osiris and the goddess of the West, (2) a stela with funeral outfit, and (3) Puyemrēʿ seated with his two wives (to whom he was not necessarily married at the same time). Most of the decoration of the walls is in relief, the good solid craftsmanship of the reign of Tuthmosis III, though for some reason the tomb has seldom been illustrated in art books.

Among the remaining tombs of the dynasty at Khôkha, which all have points of interest to offer, one may perhaps point out what is probably the smallest decorated tomb in the entire necropolis. The tomb (no. 175) is also anonymous and, with the exception of a few faded hieroglyphs, entirely deprived of inscriptions. Yet it is an interesting little monument to a man who was possibly connected with the scent industry in the reign of Tuthmosis IV. The one room of the tomb, hardly bigger than a large desk and too low for a grown-up to stand upright, has painted decoration done by two different painters, or by one painter using two different techniques for mixing his colours. On the wall to the right they

FIGURE 48
Looking into the tiny tomb TT 175.

are light and almost transparent, whereas to the left and on the rear wall the pigments seem to have been mixed with varnish. The one scene of particular interest in the tomb is a register showing various stages of the fabrication of scented unguents, from boiling the fat to steeping the aromatic herbs and wood, straining the ointment and storing it in jars. In the register above we see the visitors at the banquet crowned with lumps of unguent, while on the opposite wall the funeral procession moves slowly inwards, round the corner towards the enthroned figures of Osiris and Anubis, rulers of the world of the dead.

The tombs of Draʿ Abû el-Nagaʿ are scattered over a very large area. The hillside is here intersected by valleys, the dark openings of the tombs facing one another across the barren desert. Some forty-eight decorated tombs of the Eighteenth dynasty are known to be here, though some have vanished over the past two centuries, either because they have been totally stripped of their decoration, or because the roofs have caved in, the tombs have become sanded over and their exact location lost. This happened in other areas of the necropolis as well.

At a very early time in the dynasty, this site was chosen by a mayor of Thebes called Tetiky. In the tomb (no. 15) is a representation of Queen ʿAḥmosi Nefertere, a member of the royal family whom we shall have occasion to meet later. She was mother of Amenophis I and was considered mother of the whole dynasty, adored as a patron of the necropolis long after her death. But in Tetiky's tomb she is probably depicted during her life-time, before she was raised to divine status.

The tomb of Antef (no. 155) was known as a landmark to the travellers early in the previous century, lying half-way up the hill just where the northernmost valley was eroded into the rock. Antef was royal herald of Tuthmosis III and had probably also served under Queen Ḥatshepsut. The most spectacular scene in this now rather devastated tomb was that showing Antef about to thrust his harpoon into a ferocious hippopotamus in the papyrus thicket. Although this subject does occur in some tombs it was not very common. The beast had long since vanished from the area, and the hunt was an anachronism, the representation of which must have taken its inspiration from tombs in another place and another time. Yet as a symbolical representation it was more than adequate: the hippopotamus was evil and dangerous, and by mastering it on the tomb wall Antef would be able to master all other dangers on his way.

Because of the owner's occupation the tomb of Nebamūn (no. 17) will also be mentioned here. Nebamūn was a physician in the reign of Amenophis II whose fame was not confined to Egypt. No wonder that he had to depict the most momentous event in his career on one of the walls. We do not know whether the Syrian nobleman was taken ill while travelling in Egypt, or whether he came with the specific purpose of consulting Nebamūn. Perhaps the cup extended to him contained one of the herbal potions for which Egypt was truly famous. The reward for the treatment was costly produce from the homeland of the nobleman, including metal ingots and a silver jug.

The tomb of Nakht the gardener (no. 161) and of Wensu, whose tomb (no. A4) has only recently been properly identified, will be discussed in Chapter 6. But Draʿ Abû el-Nagaʿ was very likely the site of a tomb that, in spite of the fact that it has been reduced to fragments, is among the most frequently depicted of all the tombs in the necropolis, rivalled only by the tombs of Nakht and Menna at Sheikh ʿAbd el-Qurna.

The owner of the tomb was 'scribe and counter of grain of the divine offerings of Amūn'. His wife was called Ḥatshepsut. His own name was almost certainly Nebamūn, a very common name. His tomb was decorated at about the same time as the tombs of Nakht and Menna, both of which have no actual date written in them, but the period concerned was sometime during the eight years of the reign of Tuthmosis IV or the beginning of that of Amenophis III. Ten large fragments were acquired together by the British Museum in the 1820s, followed some decades later by an eleventh, which without any doubt at all came from the same source. Anyone who is slightly acquainted with ancient Egypt will have met the banqueting ladies, the crowds of cattle and geese, and Nebamūn spearing fish in his tiny canoe. But the paintings have not been considered as a whole before, and the tomb from which they stem has only been erroneously identified. It is quite obvious that the tomb from which the paintings came cannot be any of the tombs otherwise known in the necropolis owned by persons named Nebamūn. But this

FIGURE 49
Fragment of wall-painting from the tomb of Nebamūn now in the British Museum.

is not the end of the line of research. Some forty years ago two little fragments were sold from a private collection in Cairo. They were once part of the other half of the fishing and fowling scene, of which the right part is in the British Museum. Thus, if two more fragments have appeared, perhaps there could be others, and perhaps one would provide the vital clue.

Like most other tombs, this one must once have had registers showing agricultural activities. The fragment in the British Museum with horses and mules has remains of registers above and below, the upper one showing grain spread out either on the threshing field or in the granary. Strangely few fragments of agricultural scenes have found their way into museums and private collections, but in 1906 the Egyptian Museum in Berlin acquired a number of small pieces. These fragments could easily have been painted by the same artist who decorated the tomb of Nebamūn, judging from the way the faces and certain little details have been drawn. One of the small fragments in Berlin stands apart from the rest, not only because it depicts an unusual subject, but also because it has an excavation record, and this is what eventually brings us to consider a location for the tomb at Draʿ Abû el-Nagaʿ.

The fragment shows four men in a field who have set up a large net to catch a flock of quails desperately trying to escape their fate. The painting was found 'protruding from the lower part of a wall' in a part of Draʿ Abû el-Nagaʿ where an Anglo-German expedition worked at the turn of the century. Unfortunately a detailed report was never included in the publication, a drawing of the fragment, which was then more complete than it is now, being reduced to a mere vignette with no mention at all in the text.

During the early spring of 1985 the present writer attempted to remove rubble from some unnumbered tombs in the area concerned in the hope of finding just the tiniest clue to link up the fragment with a tomb. Unfortunately the initial investigations turned out to be abortive. Though on clearing cavities in the rock previously unrecorded tombs were discovered, these were almost completely deprived of decoration, although traces showed that they had indeed once been decorated. No names and titles had survived. The quality of the plaster on the walls did not appear to correspond to the type of mudplaster used in Nebamūn's tomb, so although one tomb was identified by a much later graffito as one of those searched by the earlier expedition, neither of the tombs was a likely candidate for Nebamūn's paintings. It is hoped that the investigations can continue at some later date and solve this puzzling problem once and for all.

The Eighteenth dynasty did not come to an end with the Amarna interlude. After Tutʿankhamūn there was the reign of Ay to come, and that of Ḥaremḥab which bridged the gap between the Eighteenth and the Nineteenth dynasties. As far as the decoration of the very few Theban tombs from the latter reign is concerned it seems more closely related to what was to come.

One of the two tombs decorated in the reign of Ay is that of Neferḥōtep (no. 49) at Khôkha. Although it is now open to visitors there is little to see, for the tomb has been lived in and the walls are blackened by smoke to the extent that it must be a disappointment to most. Yet the paintings were traced off earlier in this century, and the publication of them more than does justice to the original. New details were added to the scenes in this spacious tomb, though great care was evidently taken to make the scheme of decoration conform to what had been the norm before the Amarna revolution. But nowhere else in the necropolis do we find a representation of the tomb owner visiting the garden of the temple of Amūn at Karnak and presenting a bouquet of flowers to his wife, who accompanied him. Nor do we find the joyous occasion of returning home, and the ensuing garden party where one lady wanders out of the gate with a jug of wine in her hand. A small patch of wall has tentatively been cleaned recently and shows the original brightness of the colours. It is indeed possible with immense patience and countless pads of cotton wool to get rid of the soot of the centuries. Surely this must be one of the most urgent cosmetic jobs waiting to be carried out in the necropolis.

A tomb (no. 50) at Sheikh ʿAbd el-Qurna was also owned by a man called Neferḥotep, and the two have often been confused, though they hardly have more in common than the name of their occupant and their proximity in time. The tomb of this latter Neferḥotep, who held a high office among the clergy of Amūn, is decorated in relief and is chiefly

FIGURE 50
King Ḥaremḥab rewarding his officials and, below, the tomb owner and his wife being attended to (TT 50). Hay MSS 29844A, 194.

known for its several 'harpists' songs'. But it has a number of unusual points of interest to offer. It is safely dated to the reign of Ḥaremḥab by the fact that Neferḥotep, and two of his fellow officials, are shown receiving the coveted reward of golden necklaces from the king in the third year of his reign. This was a subject which was touched upon in the tomb of Raʿmosi and which was in particular favour in the Amarna period – one recalls the picture in one of the tombs there showing the owner of the tomb receiving golden ornaments and other gifts, including a pair of gloves. With the exception of three gloves found in the tomb of Tutʿankhamūn there is little evidence of gloves having been worn by the Egyptians, though one would probably have to look for them in scenes of archery. But it now seems that gloves could have been part of the reward 'package', for both Neferḥotep and his companions clearly wear bright yellow gloves at the ceremony. This fact has only recently been recognised from a coloured drawing done in the 1820s by Hay, for on the wall itself the colours have faded so that it is impossible to discern the difference in the colour of the hands and the rest of the body.

It has not yet become clear what effect the Amarna period had on the necropolis at Thebes. People still lived in the city, and they must have visited the tombs of their relatives and eventually themselves have found a place for a burial. Yet we have only about six tombs which can be dated with certainty to the period of about thirty-five years after the return from Amarna to the beginning of the reign of Ramesses I. When the court returned to Thebes, the normal activities in the necropolis must have been resumed. Neferḥotep was intent that his own funerary cult should be properly organised, and that special occasions should be accurately observed by those in charge. To this end he had one entire wall of his tomb inscribed with the names and dates of all the festivals to be celebrated along with summaries of the rites to be carried out and illustrations of the same. Perhaps for a while his prescriptions were heeded.

4
THE RAMESSID TOMBS
(1308–1087 BC)

The tombs of the Ramessid period (Nineteenth and Twentieth dynasties) differ radically from those of the Eighteenth dynasty. It is difficult to see how the brief Amarna episode could be responsible for a change which was strictly speaking no less a revolution than the idiosyncratic ideas of the heretic king himself. Yet the underlying ideas in tomb decoration conform to the trend which had gone before, and the Ramessid emphasis on religious orthodoxy has been considered a 'natural' development, a desperate clinging to the ideas of old, in a new unambiguous guise.

In the Ramessid tombs there is hardly any of the obvious Eighteenth dynasty symbolism left. The 'scenes of daily life', which incorporated a multitude of concepts of rebirth and resurrection, are now abandoned. No more hunting in the desert to combat evil. No more fishing and fowling in the papyrus thicket. If this subject is taken up at all, it has for some reason been transformed into representations showing the tomb owner and his wife angling from the shore of a lake or river (yet still with two fishing lines to catch the two fish at a time!). No more lavish banquets with wine and beer and unguent and music. We do have the occasional harpist or lutist with his song, and now and then a row of relatives, but usually moving along the wall like the offering bringers, not seated on mats or on chairs. The agricultural scenes are reduced

FIGURE 51
Cat slaying a serpent, the traditional enemy of the sun god. *Book of Gates* (TT A16). From Hay MSS 29851, 112.

to one or two episodes, if they are included at all. Judging from the lack of representation, viticulture would seem to have become extinct, though in actual fact this would hardly have been the case.

The basic wishes for perpetual life in the Hereafter must, however, have remained the same. The influence of Amenophis IV/Akhenaten did not have a lasting effect. But the language in which the hopes of the people were couched had changed.

One subject occurs again and again in the Ramessid tombs: scenes from *The Books of the Underworld*, especially *The Book of Gates* and *The Book of the Dead*. The books describe the appearance and organisation of the Hereafter and the creatures the deceased was likely to meet there. This includes the event of weighing the heart of the dead man against the feather of Truth and the final judgement of him before he is accorded entrance into the kingdom of Osiris.

FIGURE 52
The tree goddess dispensing her gifts (TT 158).

The tree goddess providing nourishment in the Afterlife occurred sporadically in the latter half of the Eighteenth dynasty. Along with pictures of the Ḥatḥor cow in the mountain it now becomes one of the most popular and picturesque single motifs in the tombs. The Ḥatḥor cow is shown being partly incorporated into the pink hillside, a familiar, yet august creature at the gate to the unknown. The tree goddess grows her human body from the trunk of the tree and proffers on her arms the fruits grown on her branches.

Scenes showing the office of the tomb owner were reduced to a minimum. Yet a few found occasion to give a personal touch to their monuments by adding some biographical details either in text or in representation, recording either a reward by the king; the solemn occasion when the tomb owner was installed as vizier; or a scene referring to an occupation such as weaver, gardener or inspector of workshops. But gone are the scenes of tribute bringers, arts and crafts, military activities and other duties. The reigning king does not have the same prominent position as before, contrary to royal persons of long ago, whose reputations as patrons of the necropolis had long since been established. Amenophis I and his mother, ʿAḥmosi Nefertere, who lived at the beginning of the Eighteenth dynasty, had appeared as divinities in the tombs of the reign of Amenophis III, but from the Nineteenth dynasty they become much more frequent, and other ancestral relations sometimes join them.

FIGURE 53
The Ḥatḥor cow in the mountain with a royal figure below (TT 19). From Hay MSS 29851, 221.

Few Egyptians deviated from the pattern once it had been set. It would probably not have taken the Thebans long to adapt, and to maintain that this was the only proper way to have one's tomb decorated. The chapels of the Eighteenth dynasty must have appeared somewhat 'frivolous' by comparison. Yet the ultimate purpose of tomb decoration was the same: to ensure an existence for the deceased once he had departed from this life.

In spite of their heavy subject matter, the Ramessid tombs are often delightful works of art. The colour scheme changed to include more yellow, golden colours, not only in the figures and their garments, but also in the background. Though the style of painting changed as well, the draughtsmanship did not suffer, and in many instances it seems even more elegant than before. This in particular applies to the painted tombs. Those sculpted in relief do not always achieve the same standard, especially when the sculptor exploited a new technique which had come into vogue: that of cutting relief in wet gypsum which had been applied in a thick layer to the walls. It is only possible to cut successfully into gypsum before it dries completely, and this meant that the sculptor was obliged to work without hesitation. The final coat of paint would cover a multitude of sins, but, with a few exceptions, the result is not as satisfactory as the old-fashioned method of carving the limestone itself.

The architecture of the tombs had not changed a great deal. We still have the predominant T-shaped tomb with or without pillars in the hall and/or passage. But the distribution of the scenes differ markedly from the pattern of the Eighteenth dynasty tombs, as they are almost all of a religious nature. It is by no means rare to find that the funeral procession has moved to the hall, and that the faces of pillars are taken up by scenes showing the deceased adoring a god, just as in a royal tomb. The whole system of distributing the subjects on the walls seems less rigorous than before, now that the majority of them are concerned with *The Books of the Underworld* and the tomb owner communicating with various deities.

It is more than likely, and in several cases actually proven, that an Egyptian of the Ramessid period took over a tomb from the previous dynasty and either redecorated it completely, appropriated some walls, or added his inscriptions to existing representations. If the original tomb had been left unfinished and undecorated, any trace of the first occupant may be lost. Before we pay a visit to the most notable tombs of the Nineteenth and Twentieth dynasties, it may be interesting to have a brief look at some of these re-used tombs.

There is a small tomb (no. 54) at Sheikh ʿAbd el-Qurna, originally planned by Ḥuy, a sculptor, who probably functioned in the reign of Amenophis III, which has a forecourt and a hall. A passage or inner room was never carried out. The tomb is situated in a part of the hill where painted decoration was most feasible. Ḥuy had left the front wall decorated with a representation of the funeral procession in immaculate style. For the left side wall a painted stela was chosen with offering scenes along the sides and bottom. But the remaining walls are dominated by a certain Kenro, a priest of the early Nineteenth dynasty. He carried on the decoration in the right part of the room, but incorporating and acknowledging Ḥuy's contribution. On the left rear wall Kenro offers to Ḥuy and his wife, while in a lower register Kenro and his wife offer to the Ḥatḥor cow. The right rear and side walls are dedicated to Kenro's funerary ceremonies. On the right front wall Kenro is shown libating to Amenophis I and ʿAḥmosi Nefertere as well as to Osiris, but a lower register shows Ḥuy presiding over a market scene. The crucial part of the tomb, the niche at the rear wall, belongs to the newcomer, Kenro.

This is altogether an intriguing case of co-existence in the tomb. One wonders what the relation between the sculptor and the priest could have been, and whether they could possibly have been acquainted, or even related.

In another tomb (no. 58) at Sheikh ʿAbd el-Qurna the new occupant was less considerate. Amenḥotp and Amenemōnet, temple officials in the mortuary temple of Ramesses III, encroached upon an existing tomb to the extent that the name and titles of the previous owner have not survived, and only a sketched representation of him before Amenophis III and Ḥatḥor is extant on one wall.

A magnificent tomb, also at Sheikh ʿAbd el-Qurna, known to the early travellers to Egypt, but now rarely visited, was decorated in the reign of Ramesses IX by a head of the temple scribes of Amūn, called Imiseba (no. 65). The tomb he took over had been cut in relief, but apparently only one wall had been completed. Imiseba wanted painted decoration, and he simply superimposed his paintings on reliefs, which had been lovingly thought out by a scribe called Nebamūn almost four hundred years before. A scene showing Ramesses IX burning incense before the sacred boats from the temple of Karnak was painted over a relief of Nebamūn inspecting produce.

About 194 tombs in the necropolis date to the Ramessid period. Forty-seven of them are at Deir el-Medîna, and we shall come back to these at the end of this chapter. Fifty-five of the remaining tombs are located at Draʿ Abû el-Nagaʿ, thus outnumbering the Eighteenth dynasty tombs in this area. The situation is the reverse at Sheikh ʿAbd el-Qurna where there are almost three times as many tombs of the Eighteenth dynasty, 110 as opposed to thirty-seven Ramessid tombs. At Khôkha the proportion is fairly even, thirty-two Eighteenth dynasty tombs to twenty-nine Ramessid, whereas the two Eighteenth dynasty tombs at ʿAsâsîf are overshadowed by fourteen Ramessid tombs.

Qurnet Muraʿi boasts twelve Ramessid tombs, with six from the Eighteenth dynasty. A high ranking priest in the mortuary temple of Amenophis III found the place suitable for his tomb, it being situated immediately above the temple which employed him (no. 277). The stonemasons working for Amenemōnet were not very successful in cutting a regular chamber and left it with hardly a straight line in it. Perhaps this induced the painters to leave their measuring strings at home, too. In spite of the fact that the final impression is far from neat, the tomb has some interesting scenes to show, inspired by events which Amenemōnet himself had witnessed and perhaps even organised. King Amenophis III, long since departed, was treated as a god in his mortuary temple, and like the statue of the god Amūn at Karnak he was taken out in procession with his consort. The statue of Amenophis III and his wife, Queen Teye were placed on sledges and dragged along, surrounded by priests and officials. On another wall the Ḥatḥor cow peers out of her mountain. She has company, for in front of her are placed two statues of other deceased royalty-gods, while the tomb owner is shown offering and libating to them so that they in turn would offer their protection when he himself entered the mountain.

A once worthy representative of the Ramessid tombs at Qurnet Muraʿi is in the same neighbourhood (no. 222). Now it presents a disheartening sight. The transverse hall was burnt out at some stage, leaving the mud-plaster the colour and nature of terracotta, with the colours of the paintings changed beyond recognition. The passage suffered an even more cruel fate at the hand of man, for all along the two walls squares of the decoration were cut out, chiefly the faces of the figures. These pieces are now in various collections, and one recently appeared on the art market. Hekmaʿetrēʿ-Nakht, nicknamed Turo, held a top position in the clergy of Monthu at Thebes, his wife being in charge of the god's harim. The subjects depicted in the tomb hardly present anything out of the ordinary, but the craftsmanship is sound. Any Ramessid fragments which surface in collections or on the art market should first be checked against this tomb when their provenance is sought. There is a fair chance that they may come from here.

FIGURE 54
A sad sight: fragments cut from the walls of TT 222. Some are now in museums and other collections.

At the beginning of the Nineteenth dynasty a chief steward of Amūn named Amenemōpet began work at his tomb (no. 41) at the lower enclosure at Sheikh ʿAbd el-Qurna. It was to be a grand tomb with a pillared forecourt extending in front of the entrance, for at the foot of the hill there was room enough. The low-lying situation, however, was exactly what caused the deterioration of the monument, for it has suffered greatly from damp, and the walls are very fragile. The tomb was among those visited by travellers to Egypt before 1830, being then known as the 'mystical' tomb, and in spite of its dark and gloomy appearance, it attrac-

FIGURE 55
Mourners and priests in front of a figure of the tomb owner (TT 41). From Burton MSS 25644, 95 *verso*.

ted a number of draughtsmen who attempted to copy the scenes on the walls.

It is interesting that Amenemōpet, who must certainly have been born by the end of the Eighteenth dynasty to have flourished in the reign of Sethos I, made few concessions to the conventions of Eighteenth dynasty tomb decoration. But we do have reflections of Amarna subjects in the tomb, such as the scene showing the house of Amenemōpet and people in the street acclaiming him as he arrives home in his chariot. On another wall the tomb owner is shown in a procession to the temple. The occasion of the great man's funeral brings back memories not only of el-Amarna, but also of contemporary tombs at Saqqâra near Memphis in the north, which are becoming more and more familiar to us as excavations proceed. It is in tombs like that of Amenemōpet that we shall look for close parallels to Memphite tomb decoration, although it is early days yet to define where this characteristic style of sculpture originated. The relevant Theban tombs of the early Nineteenth dynasty have not yet been adequately published, although they have been known for a long time. Their Memphite counterparts are only just beginning to emerge from the sand.

Amenomōpet included in his tomb episodes from the funerary workshop to show the manufacture of the various items needed for a perfect performance on the day of the burial. But in other respects the tomb artist appears to have taken to the new subjects of decoration: the weighing of the heart; the tree goddess; and adoration of funerary deities.

Paser was governor of Thebes and vizier to Sethos I and Ramesses II. His tomb (no. 106) emphasises his important position. Like the tomb of Amenemōpet, it was frequently visited by the early travellers, but its publication is long overdue. Its façade with niches and statues is better preserved than most. The decoration inside is in relief. On one wall Paser included a copy of the document recording his installation as vizier, one of the rare instances of biographical information which one is always searching for in the tombs but so rarely finds, particularly at this period. In addition, Paser chose a scene showing him being rewarded and acclaimed before Sethos I, and another scene recording his duties as supervisor of the workshops of Thebes, inspecting the manufacture of a statue of the king and the weighing of precious metal. Large portions of the remaining walls and pillars are taken over by funerary scenes, the tomb owner and his family adoring the deities of the Hereafter.

Piay, scribe of the accounts in the Ramesseum (mortuary temple of Ramesses II) cannot have been a top civil servant, but nevertheless he was able to have a little tomb (no. 263) cut out in the hill not far from the temple. Its chief claim to fame lies in the decoration of the entrance doorway. The left thickness of the jamb shows the couple adoring and playing draughts, and being presented with a bouquet. On the right thickness the couple recite a hymn to Osiris, whereas below a harpist plucks the strings of his instrument and sings his harpist's song, one of several recorded in the necropolis. In poetic form it repeats the wishes for the provisions in the Hereafter which the tomb owner has gone to great lengths to ensure through the texts and pictures elsewhere in his tomb.

Painted decoration was preferred by Userḥēt, a first prophet of Tuth-

FIGURE 56
A harpist with his song
(TT 263).

mosis I in the reign of Sethos I. Userḥēt was thus employed in the mortuary temple of a king who had been dead for more than two hundred years. We are at the beginning of the Nineteenth dynasty, and the painters chosen by Userḥēt for his tomb (no. 51) turned out to be true artists, both when choosing their palette and in undertaking the all important outline drawing. One of the subjects chosen was the festival procession of Tuthmosis I showing the statue being dragged along and travelling on the sacred lake of the temple.

Some ancestors were allowed a place in Userḥēt's tomb to benefit from the rites carried out. In that they were named, the magic power of the picture would work for them, too, wherever they were.

The Abydos pilgrimage was still considered an important scene to include. But it is perhaps the representation of the tree goddess and the couple sitting in her shade which is the real masterpiece in this tomb. The dark green foliage sets off the shades of pink of the sycomore figs, irresistible to the birds as well as to Userḥēt and his wife.

In the following reign of Ramesses II the small tomb (no. 341) of Nakhtamūn, head of the altar in the Ramesseum, was decorated by painters who were also master craftsmen of their time, though the architect of the tomb had hardly left them a straight wall on which to apply their design. The subjects depicted are conventional, but the painting is done with the refreshingly free flowing hand of a painter enjoying his task without aiming for perfection. A novel detail, undoubtedly based on observation from real life, is the tomb owner shown with his clean shaven skull protected by a white scarf or towel.

One of the most perfect Ramessid tombs is that of Neferronpet, a scribe of the treasury in the reign of Ramesses II, at Khôkha (no. 178). On the walls are neatly laid out a catalogue of the scenes deemed necess-

FIGURE 57
A towel put to good use (TT 341).

FIGURE 58
The tomb owner and his family waiting for offerings (TT 178).

ary for a problem-free existence in the Hereafter. We can read it as we would turn the yellowed pages of an old book. The pages have been enlarged for us and mounted on the walls of the tomb to make a complete exhibition. In the left part of the tomb we have fourteen scenes in two registers, mainly excerpts from *The Book of Gates*: the deceased, always with his wife Mutemwia, adoring divinities, their hearts being weighed in the balance at the judgement scene, drinking from a pool, playing draughts, listening to a harpist, and burning incense to Amenophis I and ʿAḥmosi Nefertere. In the right half of the hall Neferronpet, alone or with his wife, adores more gods in the upper register, whereas the lower register has a complete funerary procession to the tomb, as well as the tree goddess.

In the inner room to the left there are eight scenes of adoration of gods, including the Ḥatḥor cow in the mountain. Below, the priests are actively performing rites before the tomb owner. To the right are nine scenes, of which the upper register again shows the deceased couple before gods. This is getting slightly monotonous, but then comes the surprise: the lower register shows the tomb owner inspecting workshops with little figures milling about making beads, statues, painting, weighing metals and cooking. The building itself, which is part of the treasury of which Neferronpet was a scribe, frames the scene showing partition walls and elaborate doors.

FIGURE 59
The tomb owner inspecting a workshop (TT 178).

The rear wall of the tomb presents a most impressive sight: four rock-cut statues larger than life, in fair condition and painted in rich, warm colours, and flanked by tall bouquets of flowers.

Rather similar in style, and also at Khôkha, is the tomb of Nefersekheru (no. 296), another officer of the treasury. An unusual detail in the tomb is that the focal point of the monument, which consists only of the transverse hall, does not show the deceased and his relatives, who have been relegated to the narrow end wall on the right. It is the great god himself, Osiris, King of the Dead, who faces the visitor, flanked by two rock-cut statues of the tomb owner. Unfortunately the top half of Osiris has been removed, probably for resale to some collection. But Nefersekheru's idea was a novel one, which might have been taken up more often.

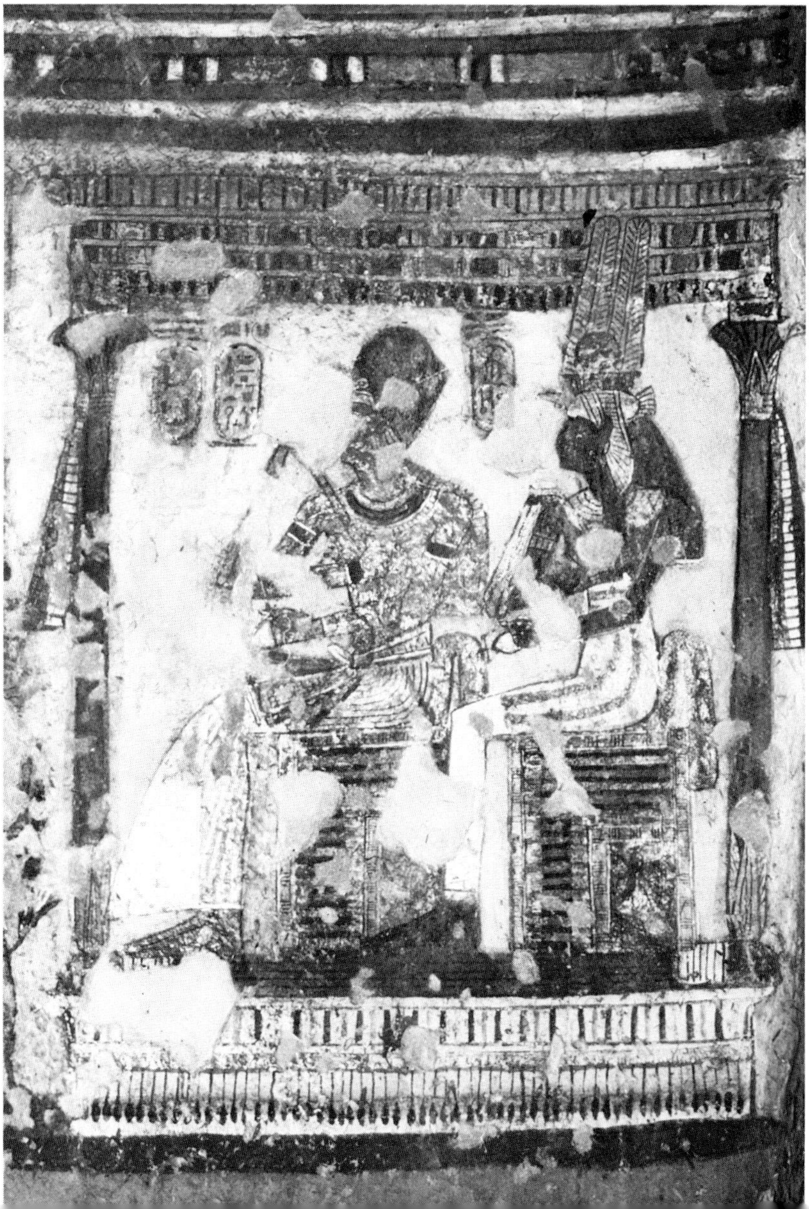

FIGURE 60
Amenophis I and his mother, Queen ʿAḥmosi Nefertere (TT 296).

We shall again pass swiftly over the ʿAsâsîf area, to which we shall return for tombs of a later period. A variety of Ramessid tombs are awaiting us at Draʿ Abû el-Nagaʿ. They betray their presence from afar. The large pyramids of mud brick which once crowned the line of tombs along the upper ridge have not all collapsed, though they no longer stand out from the surrounding hillside as they did when they were whitewashed. The northern section of this part of the necropolis, being removed from the houses, is wild and arid. The artistic gems underground make a visit worth while, although it should be added that none of these tombs is at present open to tourists.

FIGURE 61
A collapsed brick pyramid of a Ramessid tomb at Draʿ Abû el-Nagaʿ.

Before we climb the hillside we may look into a small tomb among the houses near the road (no. 16). It belonged to a priest of the deified Amenophis I, called Panehesy. The tomb is of modest proportions, but with a wealth of interesting details in its decoration. The painting is done in a bold hand. The passage behind the transverse hall has been cleared in recent years, and a shaft leads deep into the rock to a burial chamber below. The path is littered with bones and fragments of paintings provisionally stored in baskets.

An important feature in the tomb is the carrying of the enormous golden vase of Amūn in procession, followed by other objects used in the rituals. The scene takes place in front of the temple pylon. The temple is repeated on another wall, where Panehesy is shown pouring his libations. As he was an employee in the temple of Amenophis I, it is not surprising that he included a representation of himself in action in front of a statue of the king in a palanquin, along with adoration of the king and his mother, and of the boat of Sokari. This was a god of Memphite origin, who as funerary god became drawn into the sphere of Osiris and was even identified with him. This is one of the few tombs of the Ramessid period which has made room for agricultural activities, including a picture of a braying donkey carrying a basketful of grain.

FIGURE 62
The boat of Sokari (TT 16).

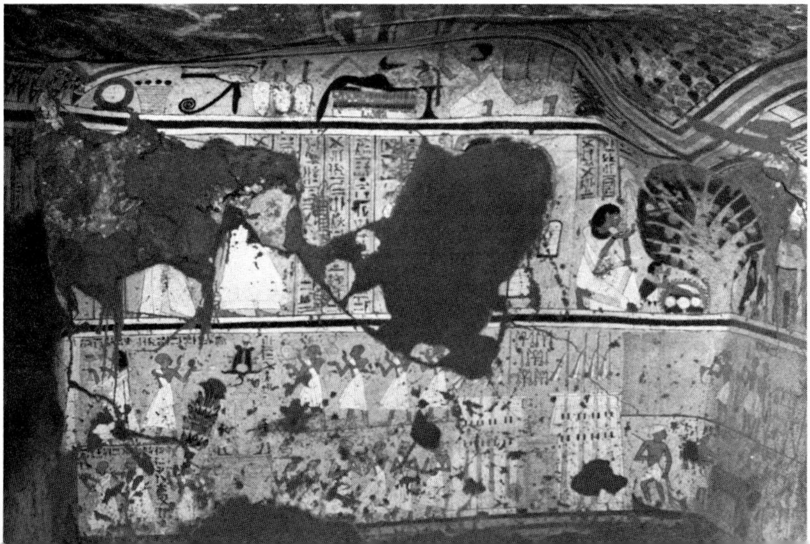

FIGURE 63
A wall in TT 16 showing the tree goddess (top right), and a procession going out of the temple.

Above the village a number of tombs of the period are clustered together. Three important tombs were cut by members of the clergy of Amūn. One (no. 157) belonged to Nebwenenef, first prophet of Amūn in the reign of Ramesses II. The decoration of the roomy pillared T-shaped tomb is carved in relief. Nebwenenef recorded his appointment in year 2 of Ramesses II as first prophet, the king and queen being shown in the window of the palace bestowing the 'gold of honour' on the official, who is all wrapped in pleated, linen garments. The tomb has some fine reliefs, including a funeral procession which has only recently come to light having been buried under at least a thousand years of habitation and debris. Nebwenenef's coffin is shown lying on a bier under a palanquin on board a boat. On top of the mummy hovers a bird, who in other similar situations is named as Isis. As the mummy is believed to be Osiris, the significance of the tableau is evident: Isis is depicted in the magic moment when after the death of Osiris her husband she conceives an heir, Horus. As Osiris was reborn as Horus, so Nebwenenef shall be reborn.

Another tomb (no. 158) belongs to Thonūfer, third prophet of Amūn, and dates from the reign of Ramesses III. A large open courtyard with reliefs on the walls precedes the T-shaped tomb, which has decoration in relief of good quality.

A fourth prophet of Amūn in the Nineteenth dynasty, named Raya, opted for painted decoration in his tomb (no. 159). The ceiling was exceptionally beautiful, having a design of ducks, pigeons and lotus flowers. Among the scenes in the tomb one showing the external view of the tomb is worth mentioning. The pyramid sits on the rocky slope of the mountain, and the row of funerary cones inserted along the façade is clearly visible.

The tomb of Niay, scribe of the table (no. 286) is an interesting representative of a smaller tomb. Pieces were cut out from the walls during World War II, but one fragment vanished long before. It has recently been identified in the collections of the Louvre. It shows two ladies in a procession which was continued in a lower register. The ladies wear a characteristic garment coloured a deep orange with white borders. If it had not been for the fairly recent damage, it would have been a very attractive little tomb with tree goddess, Ḥatḥor cow, and scenes from *The Books of the Underworld*.

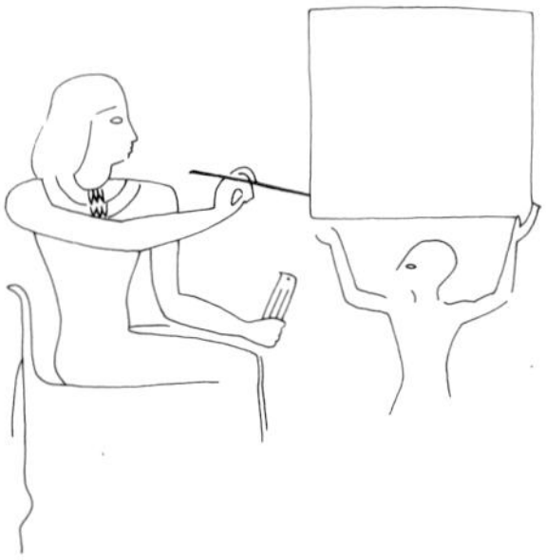

FIGURE 65
Writing on a tablet (TT A18). From Hay MSS 29816, 136.

Draʿ Abû el-Nagaʿ had many more important tombs than those known today. A traveller 160 years ago would have been shown three Ramessid tombs among many others which are no longer accessible, because their exact locations are lost. The work carried out by the early travellers will be discussed again in Chapter 6, but we shall anticipate and bring the three tombs into the context where they belong.

Scenes from the tomb of Amenemōpet (no. A18) were published by some early epigraphers and show carefully executed paintings. One of the walls takes up the scene of rewarding the tomb owner, though a royal favour is not implied. The necklaces are not the golden ones, but

FIGURE 64
Fragment of wall-painting from TT 286, now in the Louvre. Courtesy of the Louvre.

are made of flowers, and it is relatives, not royalty, who attend. Amenemōpet was chief of the scribes in the estate of Amūn. He depicted himself in office, writing a hieroglyphic text on a tablet held up by a young man. This is a highly unusual detail.

The tomb of Ḏḥutiḥotp (no. A16), leader of festivals in the temple of Amūn-Rēʿ and chief steward, was copied in great detail by Hay, who actually traced off large portions of the walls. These tracings have never been published. They are on numerous sheets of oiled tracing paper and are done in a faint pencil line, and they need complete retracing to come out in print. Apart from scenes from *The Book of the Dead*, there is a unique detail showing a horse with a serpent on its back. The significance of this is far from clear, as horses have no place in Egyptian mythology.

Userḥēt was head of measurers in the granary of the estate of Amūn in the reign of Ramesses III. His tomb (no. A17) was also copied by Hay, though only one wall was traced in facsimile. A reference in a notebook by Hay enables us to trace one fragment, showing a boat on a stand, to the collections of the Ny Carlsberg Glyptotek in Copenhagen. It would seem that other fragments survive in the Field Museum in Chicago. These latter three pieces have been somewhat drastically restored, but

FIGURE 67
The tomb owner adoring two aspects of Osiris (TT A16). From Hay MSS 29851, 129–37.

FIGURE 66
The horse and serpent in TT A16. From Hay MSS 29851, 101.

they do show persons who also occur in the tomb of Userḥēt. Along with the other fragment they are tangible evidence of the existence of a tomb which has to all intents and purposes vanished.

In the previous chapter we touched briefly on the subject of Deir el-Medîna, the workmen's village tucked away behind the hill of Qurnet Muraʿi. The village was functional from the moment the first royal tomb was begun in the Valley of the Kings by Tuthmosis I. The workmen and their families lived and died within the 7,500 square metres of the settlement. The bulk of our evidence stems from the Ramessid period, but this does not necessarily mean that the place was less operational during the first two hundred years of its history.

The male inhabitants, who worked for a ten day spell at a time in the Valley of the Kings on the other side of the mountain, spending the nights in an encampment overlooking the Valley, produced tombs and funerary equipment for themselves and their colleagues during their time off work in the royal tomb. The results are of a most unusual, dynamic character, at times masterful, sometimes just charming. Colours in the Deir el-Medîna tombs seem brighter than anywhere else in the necropolis, and the draughtsmanship less stereotyped. Yet with a few exceptions the workmen seem in their own fashion to have been most conventional in their choice of motifs for the walls of their tombs.

Owing to the lack of space the tombs are of modest proportions, but the villagers exploited the possibility of underground chambers to the full where, contrary to tradition, they did not leave the walls bare. All

FIGURE 68
A fragment of wall-painting from TT A17, now in the Field Museum, Chicago. It has been somewhat drastically restored.

the tombs have painted decoration, though jambs and architraves were sculpted. In the caves the paintings have survived beautifully. A typical Deir el-Medîna tomb would consist of an upper chapel crowned with a pyramid, the pyramidion being of limestone with sculpted decoration and having a stela set in the façade. The decoration here concentrates on the sun in the form of Rēʿ-Ḥarakhti, for the tomb owner aspired to take part in the solar cycle and thus be reborn every morning.

The shaft was most frequently excavated from the forecourt, not from inside the chapel. This chapel was partly cut into the hillside, partly built up of mud brick. In the underground chambers a vaulted ceiling was a common feature, providing yet more space for painted tableaux.

The majority of the subjects depicted in the tombs are of a funerary nature, showing the tomb owner communicating with a wide range of deities, and proceeding through the various sections of the Underworld, from the initial grand door marked 'Eternity' to the Fields of the Blessed, where he would reap his bumper crop of wheat and flax. It was Anubis himself, chief of the embalming house, who would tend his mummy, while the tree goddess would sustain him.

The family has an important role in these tombs, rows of named persons being lined up to participate in the rituals and virtually replacing the banquet scenes of the Eighteenth dynasty, or they are shown following the tomb owner in the funeral procession to his tomb. There are sporadic references to the voyage to Abydos and festivals of goddesses such as Ḥatḥor, Mut and Anukis, but above all to the patron of the village, Amenophis I, and his mother, Queen ʿAḥmosi Nefertere, and even sometimes to other deceased kings who are depicted in rows just as they are on the walls of the royal mortuary temples near by.

The decoration of one tomb stands apart from the usual scheme: that of Ipuy, a sculptor in the reign of Ramesses II (no. 217). The tomb appears to have only one decorated upper chamber, the paintings of which hark back to the Eighteenth dynasty in their subject matter. The greater part of one wall is taken up by a scene showing the manufacture of funerary equipment, including a large wooden shrine to be used in the cult of Amenophis I. The carpenters are busy fashioning furniture, while the painters put the finishing touches to two mummiform coffins and an assistant keeps the fire going under a pot of glue needed for the mummy cartonnage. Accidents happen in a workshop, and the casualties are seen to on the spot.

Adjoining subjects include fishing in the river with nets; agriculture and viticulture; and a picturesque garden with a pomegranate tree swaying in the wind and gardeners keeping the plants well watered. The laundry of the household has been taken to the river to be washed, while meat is cut up and fowl plucked for the midday meal. The tomb is a mine of information on little details of daily life, which are not depicted elsewhere, and which it is highly unusual to find in a tomb of Ramessid date.

At the beginning of the Nineteenth dynasty a certain Sennezem fulfilled his part in the village. His title 'servant in the Place of Truth' does not betray any elevated position in the village. We do not even know which craft was his, and whether he could possibly have decorated his own tomb (no. 1). But his monument is a masterpiece, and being in immaculate condition it is one of two tombs in the village open to the public.

One entire wall is dedicated to the subject of the Fields of the Blessed, the enchanted land surrounded by the blue wavy lines of water, lavishly planted with palm trees, poppies, mandrake and cornflowers, not to mention the fields depicted at the moment of harvest. The remaining walls are taken up by pictures of relatives in lower registers and scenes from *The Book of Gates* in upper registers and on the vaulted ceiling, and with a large scene showing Osiris, King of the Dead, on the wall opposite the entrance.

The tomb is of great interest, not only because of the quality of its paintings, but also because its contents were found intact about a hundred years ago. The wooden door to the burial chamber was in place, and inside were found the mummies of Sennezem and his relatives with their funerary equipment, including the following items: the sledge for dragging the coffins to the tomb; a bed painted in white with a decoration of two serpents and lions' legs; one white table and two stools; a wooden stick; a cubit rod; two pairs of papyrus sandals; figurines; loaves, eggs, dates, *dôm*-fruits; floral garlands; and about forty wooden boxes which unfortunately contained nothing. It is a sad fact that all these objects are now scattered among collections in Cairo, Europe and the United States, and that the burial can no longer be viewed as a whole.

One of Sennezem's sons, Khaʿbekhenet, preferred a monument of his own (no. 2), which he built next door. The paintings are of nearly the same impeccable quality and include subjects not found in his father's tomb. Khaʿbekhenet had more space to play with in his upper chamber as well as below ground. He made sure of depicting deceased royalty, whether patrons or not, as well as a picture of the Mut temple at Karnak with its occupants. One wonders what his connections with this locality might have been. But the most extraordinary scene in the tomb is to be found in the burial chamber. In addition to the conventional picture of Anubis preparing the mummy, the opposite wall shows the god doing the same to a giant fish. This may be taken literally as the mummy of a sacred fish, but possibly also as a reference to the significance of the fish in rebirth.

A number of tombs in the village are unusual because of their colour scheme. The majority of the tombs at Deir el-Medîna, including the ones we have already referred to, have the motifs painted on a yellow background, as it was customary in the Ramessid period, white being used for garments and certain details along with lavish use of black, red, blue and green. But some tombs have monochrome decoration, that is to say that the figures are painted in yellow on white background, with a few details such as hair and eyes added in black. The reason for this procedure has been explained by the expense, non-availability or time-consuming preparation of the colours blue and green. But it does not explain the scarce use of red, which appears mainly to have been used to outline the figures. The final effect is striking and could perhaps have been inspired by certain features of the decoration in the royal tombs, such as the very limited use of colours in some Eighteenth dynasty tombs in the Valley of the Kings (which would presumably have been inaccessible to Egyptians of the Ramessid period) and the ceiling decoration in Ramessid royal tombs, which have similar yellow figures, though on a dark, not white, background.

The tomb of Irinūfer (no. 290) should also be mentioned here because of a novel way of rendering the wigs of persons who have reached 'blessed old age'. Years do not show in the face the way the Egyptian artist was inclined to depict his model. But the painter of this tomb decided to let the greying hair speak for itself. The wigs stand out almost in negative and lend an added dignity to the wearers.

FIGURE 69
A rare representation of grey hair (TT 290).

FIGURE 70
The grandson of Inḥerkhaʿ
(TT 359).

Inḥerkhaʿ was foreman of the gang of workers in the reigns of Rames-
es III and IV. He undertook to dig two tombs, one being left unfinished,
he other showing off the talent of a master painter and draughtsman.
This latter tomb (no. 359), also open to the public, emphasises the
mportance of the family at Deir el-Medîna. Inḥerkhaʿ is surrounded
y children and grandchildren of different ages. The artist has been par-
icularly successful with the difficult subject of children, who are not
ust showed as miniature adults as elsewhere in Egyptian art. The tomb
wner holds the hand of his wife in affection, or tousles a lock of hair
f his grandson's carefully arranged curls.

Scenes from *The Book of the Dead* and other scriptures ensure the
afe passage of Inḥerkhaʿ and his family in the Netherworld. We are
hown how he will be taken by Thoth, god of the scribes, to Osiris.
He will swear not to have done anything wrong. He will pass through
he lake of fire; adore the Benu-bird of resurrection; meet the cat who
lays the giant serpent with a knife in its paw; and greet the swallow
n the hill, hoping that he himself will be the swallow in one of his
ransformations. Life underground was totally different from his
xistence in the village, busy as it was with its problems and squabbles,
ut nothing which could not be sorted out by invoking either the patron,
Amenophis I, Ḥatḥor in her mountain, or the dwarf god Bes, who protec-
ed women. In the Hereafter the challenges were of different proportions,
nd the decoration in the tomb reveals what a man like Inḥerkhaʿ had
een led to believe. Perhaps he did not quite . . . but it was better to
e on the safe side.

5
THE LATE PERIOD (1087–525 BC) AND THE END

The few tombs dating from the years after the Ramessid period and before the new powerful Nubian Twenty-fifth dynasty are almost all usurped tombs with no decoration of any consequence left, neither original nor imposed. Yet there is evidence in the form of funerary cones to suggest that two important decorated tombs of the Twenty-second dynasty once existed in the necropolis, one belonging to the second prophet of Amūn, the other to a prophet of Amūn and Monthu and pharaoh's scribe.

For the Twenty-fifth and Twenty-sixth dynasties we can now focus on the area called ʿAsâsîf: the plain stretching out between the temple of Deir el-Baḥri and the road running from north to south along the edge of the cultivation. The ʿAsâsîf gained importance as a burial ground as soon as Amūn rose to power again, backed by the Nubians. The most important event in the necropolis calendar was once more the Feast of the Valley, so frequently referred to in the Eighteenth dynasty tombs, less so in the Ramessid tombs, though the feast as such was not neglected. For some inexplicable reason it was omitted from the scheme of decoration in those days. The end station for the procession carrying the image of the god from his temple at Karnak to the other side of the river was always the temple of Ḥatḥor at Deir el-Baḥri, and the processional route cut right through the ʿAsâsîf.

In the Late Period it was thought vital to have one's tomb accessible from this processional way, and all the large tombs of the period are indeed placed with this in mind. The ʿAsâsîf soon took on the appearance of a city of tombs with narrow streets between giant walls. In their concept the tombs unite ideas from royal tombs, royal mortuary temples, the legendary tomb of Osiris at Abydos, and private tombs, combining them in a manner which is quite convincing.

The architectural plan of the larger tombs is carefully thought out and it is fairly consistent, the main elements for the lower apartment being (1) an anteroom approached at right angles to the axis of the monument; (2) an open 'sun court'; (3) an inner room with side chambers; (4) a corridor leading to the burial chamber further down. This corridor is not concealed like the shafts in earlier tombs. The decoration of the anteroom has reference to life on earth; the sun court may be either

FIGURE 71
The impressive arch and court of TT 34.

undecorated, or be concerned with *The Book of Gates*, providing access to the Underworld; and the inner rooms are dedicated to the subjects of death and solar rebirth. The ultimate objective of the tomb owner is still to be in the company of the gods and to partake of their eternal existence. *The Books of the Underworld* provide the passport. By pronouncing a statement it becomes a fact. 'You are one of the four sons of Horus', or 'You are in the entourage of Rēʿ in the day boat', and so on. Osiris, Rēʿ and Ḥatḥor are the chief deities invoked.

The ʿAsâsîf is dominated by the tomb of Mentuemḥēt, who held the comparatively lowly title of fourth prophet of Amūn, yet was obviously a very influential person during the two dynasties. The impressive brick arches of the superstructure of his tomb (no. 34) are a landmark in the plain, and the huge sunk courtyard of the monument is an awesome sight. The decoration of the inner rooms, concealed from public gaze, is in relief of a style which is characteristic of the period.

The sculptors searched tombs in the necropolis for inspiration and brought back motifs which they subtly transformed to give them the unmistakeable archaising look which we associate with the Late Period.

FIGURE 72 and 73
Two fine reliefs from the tomb of Montuemḥēt. Courtesy Cleveland Museum of Art.

To the sculptor of the tomb of Mentuemḥēt the models, from for example the tombs of Menna (no. 69) and Rekhmirēʿ (no. 100), were already some seven hundred years old. One would have thought that the tomb owner's needs and requirements might have changed, but apparently the subjects were still found useful. The temple of Deir el-Baḥri provided a scene of offering bringers and butchers. The agricultural scene relied heavily on the tomb of Menna (no. 69) and bringers of funerary outfit on the tomb of Rekhmirēʿ (no. 100). Representations of the funeral procession and the voyage to Abydos had hardly changed over the years; nor had the subjects of papyrus gathering and fishing, and Osiris and Rēʿ-Ḥarakhti are offered to as before. Attractive as all these scenes may be when carried out by a master sculptor, the inner spirit seems to have gone, and they hardly appear to be a statement of genuine funerary beliefs, merely a repetition of what had been stated so many times before.

In the case of Mentuemḥēt the reliefs have been cut up and are physically separated, some one hundred pieces being scattered in a great many museum collections. The result of research currently being carried out is anxiously awaited, for the tomb appears to be the prototype for other tombs of the Late Period with their decoration relying so heavily on inspiration from and interpretation of tombs of earlier times. The sculptor may make changes to the garments he copied, for example adding a knot where there was none, or providing the subject with a beard.

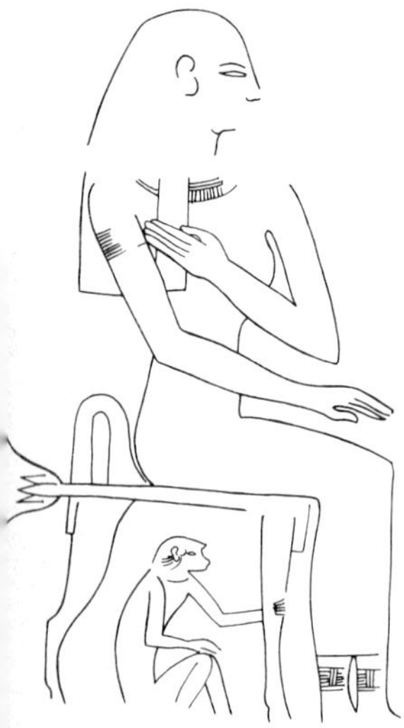

FIGURE 74
The divine adoratress and her pet monkey (TT 410).

But what really betrays the Late Period hand is the treatment of the muscles, which are considerably emphasised.

The tomb of a chief steward named ʿAnkhḥor (no. 414) was only recently incorporated in the official list of tombs, as its high number shows, although it was known to early travellers in Egypt. Though it is by no means in perfect condition, it has been impeccably restored and is now open to dedicated tourists. Among the scenes depicted is an unusual one showing a beekeeper at work.

Another recently identified tomb is that of a lady Mutirdis (no. 410) who held high office as chief lady-in-waiting to the god's wife of Amūn, Nitocris. These 'god's wives' were ladies of noble birth who achieved the status of high priestesses with considerable political influence. The tomb of Mutirdis is decorated partly in painting, partly in relief. Though rather ruined, it adds a welcome touch of colour to these otherwise stark tombs. One of the inner rooms has an astronomical ceiling, showing the sky goddess Nut swallowing the sun in the evening and giving birth to it again in the morning. This way of expressing a wish of solar rebirth was otherwise a royal prerogative.

Ibi was chief steward of the divine adoratress in the reign of Psammetikos I and thus moved in the same social circles as Mutirdis. His tomb (no. 36) is a magnificent monument, frequently drawn and described by the early travellers, though not published in recent times. A particularly interesting scene in the anteroom is reminiscent of representations of the occupation of the tomb owner in Eighteenth dynasty tombs, in particular tombs of high priests and viziers. Whether Ibi's duties actually included supervision of the same activities remains an open question. We have a whole range of crafts, from chariot-makers and woodworkers and boat-builders to sculptors, goldsmiths and potters.

In another scene in the same tomb the tomb owner has himself seated in a kiosk which is not unlike those under which royal persons used to shelter in years gone by, to enjoy a show performed by musicians and dancers. The anteroom has become a vehicle for scenes which were earlier to be found in the hall of the tomb.

The sun court, on the other hand, takes over the function of the 'passage', providing room for the funeral procession including all the traditional episodes, which were already in the Eighteenth dynasty comprised in the scheme of decoration not because it reflected actual events, but because it ensured a safe burial 'like that of the forefathers'. In the tomb of Ibi agricultural scenes and tableaux inspired by the custom of offering a bouquet at the occasion of the Feast of the Valley have also found a place in the sun court.

The inner room, which has the shape of a pillared hall, again makes reference to the Feast of the Valley, showing just how important this event had become once more.

The final large tomb at the ʿAsâsîf to claim our attention is that of Pabasa (no. 279), who was also chief steward of the god's wife. It is approached by a long flight of steps actually on the axis of the monument.

Here the funeral procession meets us in the anteroom of the tomb, while the sun court concentrates on Rēʿ-Ḥarakhti and the living persons whom Pabasa served. On studying the decoration of the pillars in the room we find yet another detail lifted from an Eighteenth dynasty tomb: the bed being prepared for the tomb owner, not only for him to rest, but also a bed on which he was destined to procreate. At least this was undoubtedly the significance of the scene in the earlier tombs. Bee keeping is repeated in this tomb, along with viticulture, netting fish and fowl, fruit gathering and, in the same room, the representation of the mummy on a couch.

Not all the high officials serving in the Late Period were buried at the ʿAsâsîf, though this is, as we have seen, where the most spectacular monuments of the period are to be found. The tomb of Raʿmosi, overseer of the treasury (no. 132) at Sheikh ʿAbd el-Qurna appears to lean more on Ramessid tombs in its decoration than on tombs from the Eighteenth dynasty. Being quite small, it is the underground burial chamber which has scenes of interest to offer, in particular scenes from the ancient *Books of Night and Day*, showing guardians posted at each of the twelve hours. The picture of the resurrection of Osiris on his couch is also influenced by a motif we have mentioned in the previous chapter. The tomb is unusual in that its decoration is entirely executed in painting. Unfortunately it has suffered in recent years through the vibrations of the heavy bus loads of traffic running close to it.

A curious fate befell a certain Espekashuti, governor of Thebes and vizier. He had built his tomb (no. 312) inside a tomb of the Eleventh dynasty. The tomb was laid out according to the pattern of an Eighteenth dynasty tomb with offering scenes and the Abydos pilgrimage on one long wall and offering scenes and the funeral procession on the other. The slabs of stone with decoration were removed and reassembled in the Metropolitan Museum of Art in New York. After being drawn and photographed the pieces were scattered among museums in the USA.

During the Late Period a great number of officials, mainly priests, had been buried in a fashion which they could neither have intended nor desired. For security reasons their bodies in their coffins were moved to mass graves in the Deir el-Baḥri area. The sites for these caches were probably chosen for the same reason for which the large tombs were located in the ʿAsâsîf below: to be near the shrine of Ḥatḥor.

FIGURE 75
A coffin from the cache at Deir el-Baḥri, now in the British Museum.

The priests and priestesses of Amūn in the Twenty-first dynasty were assembled in an ancient pit of the Eleventh dynasty just to the north of the temple of Ḥatshepsut. In 1891 no fewer than 153 coffins, ushabti boxes, statues with papyri inside and miscellaneous smaller objects were discovered some eighty yards inside the rock. To begin with, the coffins had been stacked up neatly on either side of the corridor, leaving space in the middle, but near the entrance they were in total disorder. It would seem that a high priest named Menkheper had sought out the site as a burial place for himself and his family, for they took up the innermost part of the tomb. The remaining occupants seem to have qualified merely

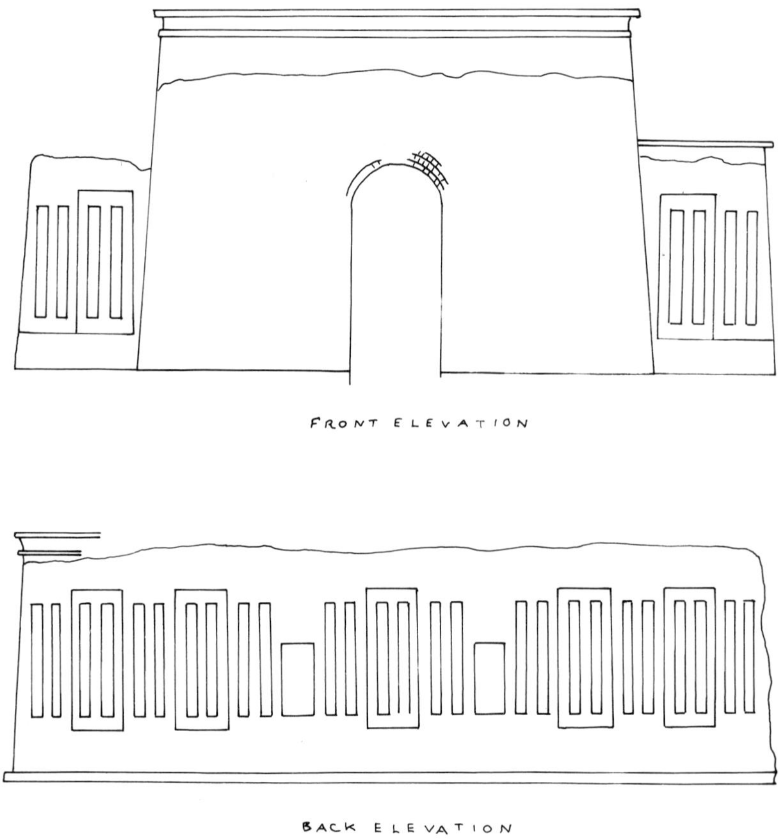

FIGURE 76
Elevational drawing and reconstruction of TT 27. From Hay MSS 29821, 84.

by being members of the clergy of Amūn, however humble: from chisellers, recruit scribes and corn scribes to singers and divine fathers.

In 1858 the priests of Monthu in the Twenty-second to Twenty-sixth dynasties had been discovered in another cache, which was actually located inside the walls of the temple of Deir el-Baḥri.

One of the latest tombs in the official list of decorated tombs is that of a certain Sheshonk (no. 27), who was chief steward of the divine adoratress in the reigns of Apries and Amasis. The tomb is now inaccessible, being located right at the bottom of the causeways leading to the temple and being on the east side of the modern road. It was mentioned by many early travellers, though little decoration of interest remains.

The last tomb on the list, chronologically, belonged to a man who was 'chief in Thebes' after the conquest of Alexander. His tomb (no. 380), of which nothing but a door jamb has been recorded, is at Qurnet Muraʿi. At Deir el-Baḥri there are remains of other Ptolemaic burials. Vital though these monuments must have been to their owners, nothing of interest has been found to tell us about them. However, numerous documents inform us of activities in the necropolis during the last few centuries BC and the inhabitants continued to entrust their bodies to the

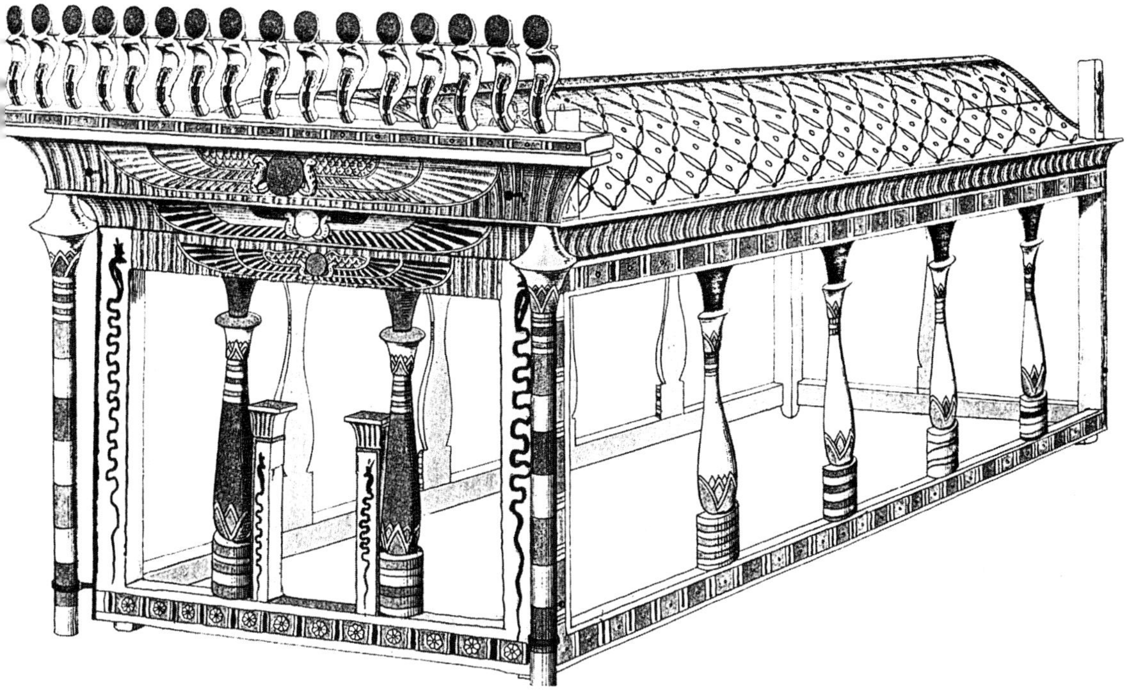

FIGURE 77
The funeral canopy as found and published by Rhind.

age-old craft of the embalmer. The Ptolemaic temple built at the northern entrance to Deir el-Medîna would have been an important centre in the life of the City of the Dead at this time, though its significance as cemetery of the capital was long since over. Thebes was by now just another town in the provinces.

Evidence for Roman burials is fairly scarce, but by a strange stroke of fate one of them was found intact. A certain Mentuemsaf, who died in the reign of Augustus, chose as a burial place for himself, his wife and some relatives an old tomb at Sheikh ʿAbd el-Qurna, which had originally been cut for a military man of the Nineteenth dynasty, but which had since been desecrated. No wall-decoration was carried out by either occupant, but Mentuemsaf had a splendid funerary canopy made of painted wood with papyriform columns supporting the roof of the structure and an elaborate architrave with winged sun's disc and cobras. It was placed in the upper chamber of the tomb, while the granite sarcophagus, which it must have sheltered during the funeral ceremonies, was placed in the lower apartments with other wooden coffins and mummy-cases. Included in the burial were mummies of a dog, an ibis, a snake; a wooden statue of a hawk; and a pot containing the fruit of the *dôm*-palm.

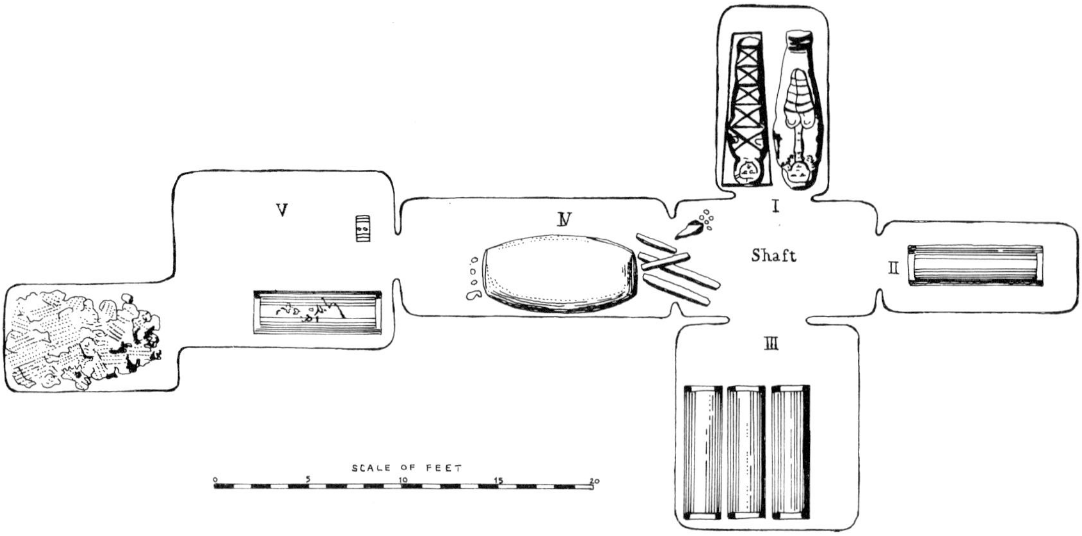

FIGURE 78
Plan of Rhind's tomb.

The mummy of Mentuemsaf was shielded by a gilt mask on which had been placed a wreath delicately shaped in gold foil on copper wire. The body was wrapped in linen with an outer shroud painted with a diagonal pattern. In the wrappings were found numerous winged scarabs in gold foil, and on the left side of the mummy was placed the inevitable papyrus scroll.

In order to take the history of the necropolis a few years further into the present era it may be mentioned that a rather similar burial with shroud and golden wreath was arranged for a man who departed this life in the nineteenth year of Trajan. But here Pharaonic burials at Thebes come to an end. Christianity took over, and a number of tombs became dwelling places for monks and hermits, some even reaching the status of monasteries (the word *deir* in Arabic meaning monastery). The Northern Monastery, Deir el-Baḥri, was dedicated to a martyr by the name of Phoibammon (including the name of Amūn, the ancient king of the gods at Thebes). Deir el-Bakhît crowned the hill above Draʿ Abû el-Nagaʿ, while a similar building was constructed on the top of Qurnet Muraʿi. The entire temple enclosure of Medinet Habu became the town of Djēme, whereas one of the tombs at Sheikh ʿAbd el-Qurna (no. 103) was turned into the monastery of Epiphanius. These Christian strongholds were later to be taken over by the Arabs, the focal points now being the tombs of the local Sheikhs, while the ancient tombs became dwellings for ordinary mortals.

Some of the original owners of tombs and pits were to undertake an unscheduled journey. During the Middle Ages their mummified bodies became much in demand for medicinal purposes, and many an ancient Egyptian found his last resting place in an apothecary's jar. It is comforting to know that the spirit of the dead person would have detached itself from its fragile shell in time.

6
REDISCOVERY

When the early travellers visited the west bank of Thebes they moored their boats under an acacia tree below the road which leads up to the mortuary temple of Sethos I, then known as 'the palace of Qurna'. Idyllic as this may seem, the traveller was faced with a somewhat daunting problem: how to visit the monuments and come out alive.

The ruins in the area of Luxor had been identified with Thebes of the classical authors by the French priest C. Sicard (1677–1726). The year 1737 found the Danish naval captain F.L. Norden (1708–42) in Egypt on a mission on behalf of Christian VI, King of Denmark. He arrived at Luxor on 11 December, mooring his boat opposite Karnak on the west bank. He must have wondered what to expect, but perhaps he was blissfully ignorant of conditions at Qurna:

> 'I got up as soon as it was day, with the design of going to see if there were not, on that side, some other remains of the ancient Thebes. I had not gone far, before I met with two great colosses [*sic*], which I took at first for those that Strabo mentions; but I had afterwards reason to be persuaded, that the colossal statues, which that author speaks of, were not the same as those which I saw.
>
> This first discovery having encouraged me, I returned on board the barque in order to get arms, and to be accompanied by those who might have a taste for being of the party. The reys [captain], who perceived our preparations, opposed them with all his might. He made use, at first, of his whole rhetorick, to endeavour to intimidate us all. Afterwards, seeing that no one yielded to his representations, he had recourse to a method, which he thought more efficacious. He swore, that, if we went ashore, he would go back with his barque, without waiting for our return. I gave him to understand, that it was a design determined on; that we would land; and if he dared go away, we should not sail to join him again, and to make him pay dearly for his insolence. This menace had an effect upon him. He drew back to entreaties that we would not land, at least out of respect to him. "If good fortune, said he, favours you sufficiently to escape the danger; yet you put me in the greatest peril in the world for the future. The people of the country will never pardon me; and when hereafter I shall have occasion to come here again, and to go on shore, they will murder me without mercy, for having brought you into their country, from whence they will certainly think that you have carried away treasures." I was too much accustomed to such sort of discourses to submit to them. But as I perceived that the time passed away, and that I should want a good deal to make my researches, I was hesitat-

ing on the part I should take: when the janissary [Turkish soldier] began to threaten the reys, and immediately went on shore with me. Some of our people followed us, and we went across the plain, taking for our guides the two colosses of which I have already made mention.'

They wound their way along the wheat fields and the canals to the colossi of Memnon, and here we find the first mention in modern times of the private tombs, although their purpose was misinterpreted:

'[The colossi] are both made of diverse blocks of a sort of sandy and greyish stone, which seems to have been drawn from some of the grottoes, that one remarks, in great numbers, in the neighbouring mountains.'

Norden sat down quietly and drew the colossi while his party spent the time in violent argument with the local sheikh and other inhabitants who had come to inquire about the strangers. Having finished his drawings he went for a walk along the mountains and actually entered several of the 'grottoes'. There is no mention of any wall-decoration, nor is there a word about the tombs at Deir el-Medîna, which he must virtually have stepped over when he visited the Ptolemaic temple next door.

FIGURE 79
The site of the Theban necropolis as drawn by Pococke.

He made it safely down to the river where he was met by a very relieved 'reys':

> 'He congratulated us on our happy return, and told us that though he had navigated more than twenty years upon the Nile he should never have ventured to land in this place: the inhabitants had such a character of being villains . . . These people occupy, at present, the grottoes, which are seen in great number in the neighbouring mountains. They obey no one, they are lodged so high, that they discover at a distance if anyone comes to attack them. Then, if they think themselves strong enough, they descend into the plain, to dispute the ground; if not, they keep themselves under shelter in their grottoes, or they retire deeper into the mountain, whither you would have no great desire to follow them.'

By a strange coincidence another famous traveller followed in Norden's footsteps just a few days later. R. Pococke (1704–65) was on a tour of Egypt and the Middle East, but the two travellers never met. Pococke was fortunate enough to have acquired a letter of introduction to the sheikh at Qurna, and he was offered full protection during his sightseeing. His published description is accompanied by a very charming, though rather fanciful panorama of Qurna:

> '[The sheikh] came to the boat and conducted me to his house marked A . . . [He] furnished me with horses, and we set out to go to Biban-el-Meluke [the Valley of the Kings] and went about a mile to the north, in a sort of street, at each side with the rocky ground about ten feet high had rooms cut into it, some of them being supported with pillars; and, as there is not the least sign in the plain of private buildings, I thought that these in the very early times might serve as houses, and be the first invention after tents, and considered as better shelter for wind, and the cold of the nights. It is a sort of gravelly stone, and the doors are cut regularly to the street.'

On the return from the Valley of the Kings Pococke 'observed in the plain to the north, many entrances into the rocks, which probably were of the nature of the grottoes I observed on each side of the way as I came.'

It is possible to identify two of the tombs Pococke saw, for in his publication he gave very neat plans of them. They are the two Saite tombs which now have the numbers 33 and 37. He includes a page of description of the architecture, the walls much damaged by fire and the bones lying about, but he takes the tombs to be the 'apartments' of the living, dug under the palaces of the kings (by which he meant the mortuary temples). However, it is of great interest to find here the first mention of a decorated private tomb.

Next man on the stage was J. Bruce (1730–94), a Scottish traveller, who arrived at Qurna on 7 January 1769. A generation had lapsed, but the attitude of the local inhabitants towards visitors had not mellowed. The tombs were held by Arabs who were fighting even other Arabs living in the plain. Bruce, who also mistook the caves in the mountains for private dwellings ('the first habitations of the Ethiopian colony which built the city') tells that:

> 'A number of robbers who much resemble our gypsies, live in the holes of the mountains above Thebes. They are all out-laws, punished with death if elsewhere found. Osman-Bey, an ancient governor of Girge, unable to suffer any longer the disorder committed by these people, ordered a quantity of dried faggots to be brought together, and, while his soldiers took possession of the face of the mountain, where the greatest number of these wretches were, he then ordered all their caves to be filled with this dry brushwood, to which he set fire so that most of them were destroyed; but they have since recruited their number, without changing their manners.'

It is no wonder that so many walls were found to be damaged by fire It was not always the smoke from the cooking that was responsible.

In the late 1770s C.S. Sonnini, the French naturalist (1751–1812) made a vain attempt to get to see some tombs, but he was put off by the local inhabitants who descended on him like vultures:

'The Arab Sheikh of Luxor urged me not to delay my departure; but I still wished to cross over to Gournei, which was on the west bank, in order to see the part of the ancient city of Thebes that was on that side of the Nile. This was reckoned to be the most difficult spot to land in Thebaïs, on account of the multitude of robbers by whom alone it was inhabited. I had heard the kiaschef [Turkish officer] of Kous say, that he would not venture to travel there, even with his little party of soldiers . . . The place where I landed was planted with gum acacias. Although the village was at no great distance from the river, as it was the resort of the most formidable banditti, I followed the advice of the sheikh of Luxor, and requested the sheick of Gournei, for whom I also had a letter from Ismaïn, to come himself to the water-side. He immediately complied with my request, and conducted me to the meanest, the most frightful, and most miserable place in appearance I ever beheld. The badly built mud huts, of which it consists, are no higher than a man, and have no other covering than a few leaves of the palm tree. And, as for the inhabitants, never did I see such ill-looking wretches. They were half black, and almost entirely naked, part only of their body being covered with miserable rags, while their dark and haggard countenance was fully expressive of their ferocious disposition. Following no trade, having no taste for agriculture, and, like the savage animals of the barren mountains near which they live, appearing to employ themselves solely in rapine, their aspect was not a little terrific . . . My companions, whose imagination had been struck by all the accounts they had heard of this truly detestable place, appeared very uneasy; the Syrian interpreter, as cowardly as he was wicked, cried from fear; they all blamed me loudly, and considered our destruction inevitable, when they saw me seated upon the sand in a middle of a dozen of these rascally fellahs, pulling out my purse every moment, and paying their own price to all those who brought me idols or antique medals. I thus made a pretty ample collection of fragments of antiquity; and I must say, in justice to the inhabitants of Gournei, they displayed as much integrity and fairness in these little bargains, which employed us a great part of the day, as if they had been the most honest people in the world.'

Sonnini paid a brief visit to some of the standing monuments, including the colossi of Memnon, but most of them he saw only at a distance:

'I could have wished much to visit some spacious excavations, hewn out in the rock, at a league to the westward of Gournei, which were the tombs of the ancient monarchs of Thebes; but I could find nobody that would undertake to conduct me thither; the sheick himself assured me that the inhabitants of Gournei being at war with those of the neighbouring villages, some of whome they had recently killed, it would be highly imprudent to expose myself with guides taken from among them, and who, far from affording me any sort of protection, would infallibly draw upon me the revenge of their implacable opponents.'

The 'spacious excavations' would be the tombs in the Valley of the Kings

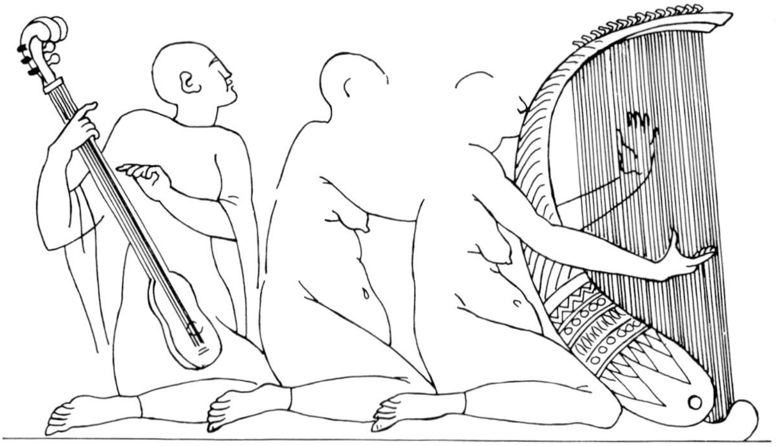

FIGURE 80
Musicians in TT 65 as copied by Denon.

on the other side of the mountain. The private tombs remained th battleground of the Arabs in search for antiquities.

Twenty years later the members of Napoleon's expedition in 1799–1800 had better luck. Due to their military escort and the fact that the paid well for the objects brought to them, including (wall-?)paintings they were assured safe conduct at Qurna. They found many of the tomb in good condition, and said that only those with easy access had suffere where previous visitors had attempted to cut out reliefs and painting to bring them to Europe, leaving behind fragments scattered on th ground.

Among the tombs they entered was no. 65. Strangely enough this popular tomb which is still in a good condition, has never been adequatel published but one scene was drawn by D. V. Delon (1747–1825), a member of the expedition. The tombs of Min (no. 109), of Neferḥote (no. A5), and probably of Puiemrēʿ (no. 39) were also among those seen but the epigraphic results were meagre. Due to the lack of time fe drawings were made, and instead copies of insignificant fragments collected from the floor were thought worthy of inclusion in the final splendid publication.

The brave members of the campaign were always knee-deep in mummies, being hardly able to disentangle their feet from the mass of broke bones and coffins. But they became used to it. The greatest hazard wa the risk of fire. In order to be able to distinguish anything at all insid torches were brought in, but the merest spark straying onto a mumm case would cause a holocaust. The Arabs used to collect piles of discarde mummies at the entrance to their caves and set them alight. The fir burnt all night.

E.F. Jomard (1777–1862) was responsible for writing up the note taken in the tombs for the *Description de l'Égypte*, published in 1809–22 The types of burial and the subjects depicted on the walls are discussed but the author could not resist including lengthy accounts of the horror which may befall the traveller. Some members of the party were strande deep inside a tomb in pitch darkness when a crowd of bats extinguishe their two candles. A shorter version of the visit to the tombs was published as early as 1800–1 by another participant, L.M. Ripaul (1775–1823).

The next glimmer of light in the darkness surrounding the early modern history of the tombs is provided by W. R. Hamilton (1777–1859), the English diplomat, who was secretary to Lord Elgin and superintended the shipping of the Elgin marbles from Athens. After the departure of the French from Egypt in 1801, Hamilton was sent out by Lord Elgin. His *Aegyptiaca*, published in 1809, contains in all seven pages on the tombs, described in such detail that it is possible to identify some of them with known tombs. Hamilton visited Wensu's tomb (no. A4), and possibly also that of Sennūfer (no. 96) with the famous scene showing the temple garden with the gate of Amenophis II. Tomb no. 65 was naturally included in the itinerary. Hamilton's records show his keen eye for details which, because of the early date of the observations, is of great value to scholars today.

Silence again surrounds the necropolis until 1815–16 and the following winters when tourists began to venture south. Visits to Egypt had previously been confined mostly to the Delta and Cairo en route to and from the Holy Land. But the overland route to India went via Quṣeir on the coast of the Red Sea. Those who had time to spare would occasionally make a detour to Thebes. Many diaries and letters home mention an encounter with the Europeans who were soon to settle down at Thebes.

Mohammed Ali (1769–1849), an Albanian in Turkish service and ruler of Egypt since 1816, had supreme right to excavations in the country, but he could extend a *firman*, or permission, to foreigners. The local inhabitants needed no firman for looting, but their need for secrecy restricted their movements. If a villager came across an unspoilt tomb, he would not want to share his find with too many others, but technical difficulties might get in the way and make the task of 'clearing' too hazardous. In this case the excavation spot would be sold to a foreigner who – with the firman in hand – would be able to exploit it to his own benefit. The pasha, however, was none too generous with the firmans. E. de Montulé gave instructions to future archaeologists for obtaining a firman in an appendix to his book about his travels in Egypt in 1818:

'Concerning those who dig for discoveries.

The mode of proceeding to search after antiquities, and transport the most precious relics from Egypt is thus accomplished. Arrived at Cairo, the consul of your nation introduces you to Mr Bangos, who presents you to the Pacha; you then explain the motives that have brought you, and make it appear that the enterprise may prove of utility to the government. This done you receive the *Firman*, or authority, which purports that all Bays and cachefs must, to the utmost, unite in forwarding your views; besides which you have a soldier completely armed to accompany you, when all that remains is to purchase presents, such as sabres, pistols, and guns of value to distribute as occasion may offer.

Possessed of these means it would appear that you had liberty to dig up Egypt itself; but only proceed to attack a pyramid, or temple, the island of

Phile, &c &c; and you will find such an attempt impossible; a single stroke of the axe had previously made such monuments the exclusive property of M. Drovetti, M. Salt, &c &c, each being in possession of his firman, which is known to the Cachef and the Arabians, wherefore it is necessary to find some structure which had hitherto escaped the research of the curious.'

In 1816 the English painter and diplomat H. Salt (1780–1827) was posted to Egypt as consul general, and, along with his French counterpart B. Drovetti (1776–1852), he was soon to become an important figure at Thebes, the two virtually taking possession of the territory. Salt's diplomatic duties, and the plague that haunted the big cities at intervals, kept him in the north for the greater part of the year, but Yanni, his agent, worked for him at Thebes in his absence. Yanni, whose full name was Giovanni d'Athanasi (1799–1850+), was a mere lad of eighteen when he first came to Thebes in 1817, but he was to become a loyal servant to Salt during the next decade. He had a house in the necropolis near the tomb of Nakht (no. 52), where he lived until 1835, and he acted as a host to many English travellers who came to work there.

The famous strong man Egyptologist G.B. Belzoni (1778–1823) was also periodically in Salt's service at this time, and although his greatest achievements are connected with the tombs in the Valley of the Kings and the temples, he also discovered and entered a number of private tombs. His *Narratives* of his life in Egypt became something of a best-seller in the 1820s. One Sarah Atkins re-wrote it for young readers, inserting a dialogue between an adult and two youngsters avid for knowledge, and including tinted illustrations. This is one of the earliest books on ancient Egypt specifically written for children.

In the late summer of 1817 the visitors to the necropolis included C.L. Irby (1789–1845) and J. Mangles (1786–1867), commanders in the Royal Navy, and Colonel J. Straton (d. 1840). Irby and Mangles wrote meticulous letters home which were published a few years later in the form of a diary. Straton composed an article in *The Edinburgh Philosophical Journal* of 1820. Irby and Mangles, who had the previous summer helped Belzoni dig out the temple of Abu Simbel when the local work-force failed him, had Belzoni himself as a guide, and they left a vivid account of the situation in the necropolis at that time, eighty years after Pococke had first described a private tomb. The local residents were no more helpful than they had been then:

'We devoted this day [18 August] to visiting the tombs of Gourna; and Mssr. Beechey [secretary to Salt] and Belzoni having been employed for months by Mr. Salt, in digging and making excavations in various directions among the rubbish of ancient Thebes, and particularly at Gourna, were the best guides we could possibly have. It is customary with the natives to deceive travellers, and tell them that they have seen all, before they have inspected half; and it was precisely this trick they played on Mr. Irby and myself on our former visit. They have not been unmindful of the eagerness with which travellers inquire after objects of antiquity; especially the papyri, which are generally found under the arms or between the legs of the mummies, and the demand for which has been so great of late, in consequence of an opposition between the French party, employed by Mr. Drovetti, and the English, employed by Mr. Salt, that they now sell for thirty, forty and fifty piasters each, whereas, formerly, you could get them for eight or ten. About a dozen of the leading characters at Gourna, that is, the greatest rogues in the place, have headed their comrades, and formed them into two distinct parties, or resurrection men, designating them the French and the English party; these are constantly occupied in searching for new tombs, stripping the mummies, and collecting antiquities. The directors have about three-fourths of the money, and the rest is given to the inferior labourers. They dread lest strangers should see these tombs, which to them are so many mines of wealth, and should commence digging speculations of their own – hence the care of the Gourna people in concealing them. It would be endless to describe all the intrigues which are carried on; or the presents given to the Defterdar Bey, the Agas, the Cashiefs, to attach them to the one or the other party.'

FIGURE 81
The musicians now in the Bankes collection as seen *in situ* by Straton (he reversed the positions of the two ladies on the right.)

One of the tombs the two naval officers visited is of particular interest because its location is no longer known. Colonel Straton entered the same tomb shortly afterwards and even sketched one of the scenes on the walls: a group of musicians with their instruments. The scene with the orchestra was not to remain on the wall for long, for the following year it was removed by W.J. Bankes (1787–1855), the English collector

FIGURE 82
A harpist from a fragment of wall painting in the Bankes collection.

then travelling in Egypt. He had it sent to England in 1821 along with four more fragments of wall-painting from the same tomb. They remain in the Bankes collection at Kingston Lacy and have only recently been identified by the present writer with the scenes described by Irby, Mangles and Straton. A relief from the tomb of Neferḥotep (no. 50) with the beginning of the festival calendar inscribed over one of the walls in the tomb was also included in the shipment.

A major attraction in the necropolis were the mummy-pits. They were scavenged by the Arabs who hoped to find treasures and papyri among the bodies and who cared little about the destruction they caused.

> 'It is impossible to conceive a more singular and astonishing sight than this,' Irby and Mangles write. 'Imagine a cave of considerable magnitude filled up with heaps of bodies in all directions, and in the most whimsical attitudes; some with extended arms, others holding out a right hand, and apparently in the attitude of addressing you; some prostrate, others with their heels sticking up in the air; at every step you thrust your foot through a body or crush a head. Most of the mummies are enveloped with linen, coated with gum, &c., for their better preservation. Some of the linen is of a texture remarkably fine, far surpassing what is made in Egypt at the present day, and proving that their manufacture must have arrived at a great degree of excellence. Inumerable fragments of small idols are scattered about; some are of stone, some of baked earthenware, and others of blue pottery. Except as being so old and extraordinary an exhibition, few of the common tombs are worth seeing as none of them are ornamented in any way whatever . . .'

Although the Arabs did their best to wreck the tombs it sometimes befell the Europeans to discover an unspoilt tomb or mummy-pit. The object of the exercise was still to provide antiquities which could be handled and sold, but some excavators took the trouble of giving a brief description of the tombs as they found them. These were, however, rarely in the state in which the Egyptians of the New Kingdom had left them. Subsequent ages had re-used the convenient caves, filled them with mummies, and blocked them up:

> After this wall of brick-work has been penetrated [writes Yanni] the explorer has to encounter a door of wood, which being in like manner removed, he beholds the mummies in a double line, ranged side by side to each other, with their hands and feet alternatively in juxtaposition, in order to take up less room. Appertaining to each of these mummies the following articles are generally found, viz.: – a wooden idol with its pedestal, being of the same form as the mummy to which it belongs; a wooden case containing the intestines of the deceased, arranged in four parcels; a wooden tablet with designs and hieroglyphics, generally well executed; and lastly, another case, containing porcelain idols of various sizes, some of which are very neatly made, and others of more ordinary execution. When a tomb is sufficiently large all these objects are found arranged about the mummy to which they

appertain, whilst in the smaller tombs these things are placed upon the mummies themselves.'

Yanni had more opportunity than most to find undisturbed tombs, and he did. But he was never anxious to show his finds in their pristine state to others. If he had, we might have been better informed as to the appearance of the burials.

The French traveller and mineralogist F. Cailliaud (1787–1869) arrived at Thebes in 1818 and returned on several occasions during the following years. He began copying wall-paintings in the tombs, and later published a large volume on the arts and crafts of ancient Egypt. The plates – there is no text – are all hand-coloured. Although they are by no means facsimiles, they are not a bad effort in the very early days of epigraphy. In 1822 Yanni had just re-discovered the beautiful tomb, seen by Napoleon's team, which now has the number A5. The tomb itself can no longer be located. Cailliaud persuaded Yanni to allow him to copy certain scenes on the walls, which he duly did.

'But now see how M. Calliot [*sic*] repaid me for all my kindness. Not satisfied with having copied to his heart's content whatever caught his fancy, he sent a messenger to Luxor, on the opposite bank of the river, to procure some iron tools, with which he forthwith set to work, detaching the crust of the wall into pieces which he began sending to his house. My Arabs, who were working in the excavations not far from the spot, having recognised the embellishments of the tomb forced them away from the men who were carrying them off; and one of them without loss of time, hurried to the tomb demanded of M. Calliot of whom he had obtained permission to take away the embellishments in this manner. On this enquiry, M. Calliot seized a piece of iron and threw it at the head of my Arab, who had come to warn him of his error; but the latter without being disconcerted, answered his attack in the same fashion, snatching from him at the same time all his implements, as well as the designs which he had just been detaching from their places, and which he brought to me. I was almost out of my senses on learning the ungenerous manner in which this gentleman had requited me of my civility; but out of pure pity I forgave him. It is almost inconceivable how he could have brought himself to publish anything relating to facts which do him so much discredit; I can only account for it by supposing that he did not expect that he whom he had so impudently calumniated would one day have an opportunity of replying to him.'

Calliaud must have succeeded in spiriting away one of the fragments, for it came with other items from his collections to the Louvre in Paris. Yanni was clearly very upset, but perhaps more because of the abuse of his hospitality than over the actual removal of the fragments. It was probably around this time that Salt, or more likely Yanni himself, stripped another tomb of its decoration. Large fragments from the tomb of Wensu (no. A4) were added to the Salt collection later to be bought by Champollion on behalf of the King of France, and thus also came to the Louvre. Yanni had already removed substantial fragments from yet another tomb. These paintings are now among the main attractions of the Egyptian galleries in the British Museum, but the tomb from which they came has not yet been identified (cf. above, pp. 59ff.).

Among the 'cowboys' in Egypt at this time was G. Passalacqua (1797–1865), an Italian who had come to Egypt as a horse-dealer. He found excavation a more lucrative business. In 1823 he came upon a tomb in the area near the temple of Deir el-Baḥri (see above, p. 24).

The objects from the tomb, along with others from the Passalacqua collection were acquired by the King of Prussia for the Berlin museum of which Passalacqua was duly made the keeper. He had made the sale conditional on his appointment. In his catalogue, published in 1826, Passalacqua includes three pages on the tombs with decoration and the mummy-pits, and he describes a spectacular find of his own: a corridor cut some one hundred and fifty feet into the mountain and crammed with coffins. Some bodies had been buried with the tools of their trade: a painter's palette; a scribe's palette with red and black ink; a bow and arrows; a measuring rope; a key; a fishing net; a hoe; and so on. Large boulders had crashed down and blocked the passage fifty feet from the entrance. Passalacqua squeezed through only to find that the tomb had been robbed and burnt through an entrance at the other end.

Although the necropolis was a hive of activity at this time, publications were scarce, and even a few pages were a step forward. Passalacqua made an interesting observation about the mummy-pits he had stumbled across. All of them had been robbed, and most were blackened by fire and full of fragments of mummies and burnt coffins. The robbers had set fire to the lot, for only items which survived the fire were worth having, namely gold and semi-precious stones. If Passalacqua is right, these robberies must have taken place before the value of papyrus scrolls was realised. He blames the destruction on Persian invaders.

Over the following century the necropolis was to remain the battleground for treasure seekers. Not only objects but also numerous fragments of wall-decoration were taken from the tombs and brought to private and public collections abroad. The scars on the walls and the fact that there are more than 160 fragments of wall-paintings alone in museums and other collections bear witness to this fact. Many more are presumably in unknown private collections abroad. It is worth noting that there is not a single fragment of a Theban painted tomb in the Egyptian Museum in Cairo, and the only piece in the Luxor Museum was originally collected from the debris of a tomb for restoration. But with the arrival of Wilkinson at Thebes serious scholarly work began.

J. G. Wilkinson (later knighted) (1797–1875) was to have made a career in the army, but in his school days he had already taken an interest in ancient Egypt. At that time attempts at solving the mystery of the hieroglyphs had been carried out for some years in England and abroad. Wilkinson gathered what information he could on the subject and in 1821 left for Egypt, where he was to stay for twelve years continuously.

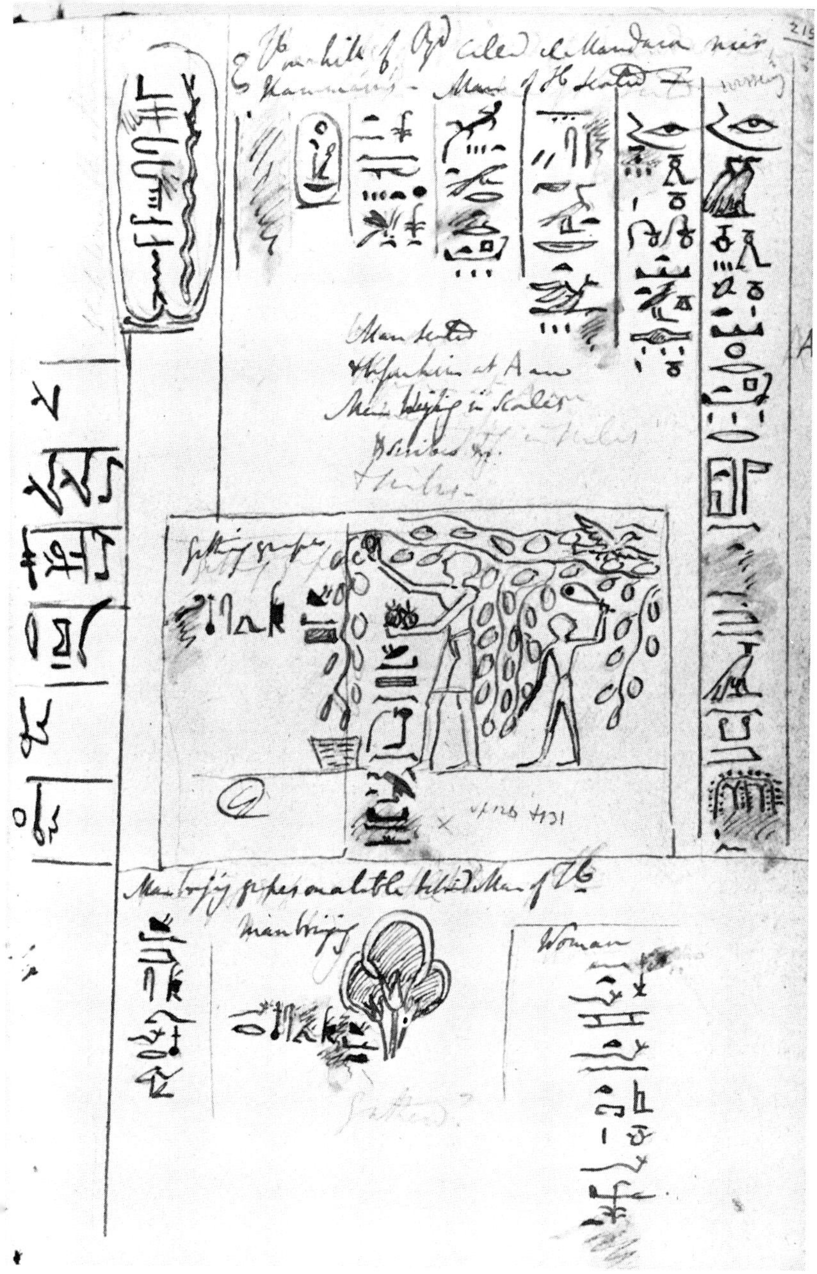

FIGURE 83
A page of Wilkinson's notebook referring to TT A24. MS V. 215.

mainly at Thebes. In 1822, when Champollion announced the decipherment of the hieroglyphs, Wilkinson had arrived at very nearly the same results.

Wilkinson settled himself high up on the hill of Sheikh ʿAbd el-Qurna in the ruined tomb of ʿAmethu, vizier of Tuthmosis III (no. 83). An extension of mudbrick was built in front, and the house was known as 'Wilkinson's castle'. His studies of the *Manners and Customs of the Ancient Egyptians*, first published in 1837, was a mine of information chiefly drawn from the scenes on the walls of tombs and temples, combined with the author's observations of the daily life of the modern Egyptians. The majority of the illustrations are freehand copies, and therefore not exact by modern standards, but there are so many of them, and so much has been damaged, if not completely destroyed, since they were made, that they can still be consulted with benefit. The work was a magnificent effort, and it ran into several editions. The fifty-six volumes of Wilkinson's manuscripts, folders and notebooks are an even greater treasure cave for scholars, for much of the material was not included in the publication. The manuscripts have now been handed over to The National Trust and deposited in the Bodleian Library in Oxford. Parts are available on microfiche.

The 1820s were the great days of pioneer epigraphy, but the high quality of some of the art work has often been underestimated. One of the reasons is that for technical reasons plates had to be re-drawn and engraved for printing, and much of the original quality was lost during the proceedings. In those days tracing paper was of a poor quality and only consisted of semi-transparent oiled sheets. Large quantities were needed, and inside the corridors of the tombs lighting conditions must have been appalling. Nevertheless very accurate tracings were made by some of the artists. The *camera lucida* was a great help providing an alternative drawing technique: a prism fixed on a stand projected the picture from the wall through a lens and onto the drawing board. The tracing could thus be carried out on heavier paper and on a more manageable scale. Sometimes these drawings were enhanced with watercolour.

As far as epigraphic work in the tombs is concerned, along with Wilkinson, Burton and Hay are the most significant contributors. They often worked side by side, and in true scholarly spirit there seems to have been no unseemly rivalry among them. All three were entirely independent of government support and had private means. J. Burton (1788–1862) came of a family of architects, although he himself had chosen mineralogy. He came to Egypt to undertake a geological survey of the country for Mohammed Ali. Meeting with Wilkinson gave him an appetite for archaeology. He came to Thebes in 1824 and returned again in 1830–5. With his *camera lucida* he drew a great number of scenes

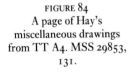

FIGURE 84
A page of Hay's miscellaneous drawings from TT A4. MSS 29853, 131.

in the tombs, and took detailed notes. R. Hay of Linplum (1799–1863) was helped in his work by a number of other artists and was thus able to copy on a large scale. Hay had entered the navy at the age of thirteen. This gave him a taste for travelling, and in his teens he had visited the Middle East and climbed Pompey's pillar. He was interested in ancient civilisations and was adept at drawing, and it was not surprising that Egypt became the outlet for his talents.

Hay first passed Thebes early in 1825 on his journey upriver to Abu Simbel. On 11 October that year he returned and settled down in the temple of Medinet Habu where the party stayed until February of the following year. After a spell in Cairo they returned to Thebes once more on 15 May, in the beginning pitching their tents on the river bank. Later they moved into Yanni's house and immediately set about their epigraphic work. This kept them busy until January 1827. After work at Abu Simbel Hay came back to Thebes in November, and then he left for England. During his second expedition to Egypt 1829–34 he spent six weeks at Thebes (19 October – 8 November 1832) collating his old drawings. The last sojourn took place from 31 January – March 1833 when Hay stayed in Wilkinson's house on the mountain.

The drawings by *camera lucida* done by Hay and his assistants are excellent, and their tracings are very nearly up to modern standards. These tracings have never been published, being drawn in a faint pencil line and on numerous sheets of paper. By re-tracing them and reducing the drawings it is nevertheless possible to obtain results which are superior to those of early epigraphers in general. The Burton and the Hay papers are now housed in the British Library in London. The two epigraphers had clearly intended to publish them after their return from Egypt, and what a contribution to science that would have been. But apart from Hay's sketches of Cairo and Burton's collection of hieroglyphs, the volumes were never edited and printed, and only selected plates are known to the public.

When Hay and Burton arrived at Thebes in 1830, extensive work had been carried out in their absence by a Franco-Italian expedition, headed jointly by Champollion and Rosellini. The path of J.F. Champollion (1790–1832) to Egyptology had been straight. At the age of sixteen he had read a learned paper to the Grenoble Academy claiming, correctly, that Coptic was a descendant of the ancient Egyptian language. Later he conveyed his enthusiasm for the subject to his sovereign, and he was appointed keeper of the Egyptian collections in the Louvre, opening to the public in 1827. Part of the collection had been acquired from the collection of Salt sold in Leghorn in 1825. In Italy Champollion met I. Rosellini (1800–43). Rosellini had gone from the study of Hebrew to being professor of Oriental Languages at the University of Pisa. The two scholars immediately became friends and in 1828 found themselves in Egypt with a number of draughtsmen and other assistants, backed by their respective governments. They spent two and a half months of the hottest season of the following year recording scenes in the Theban tombs. The results of Champollion's work were published posthumously in 1835–47 in four monumental tomes, including no less than 446 plates. Rosellini was able to see some of his efforts in print. Nine volumes, most at an equally gigantic scale, appeared in 1832–44, containing 395 plates. Not surprisingly many illustrations in the two publications are duplicated. The drawings as they appear in print are actually inferior to original drawings and tracings by Hay and Burton, and much of the style of the Egyptian reliefs and paintings is lost in the attempt to make them complete and attractive. But perhaps the copies by Hay and Burton would have suffered a similar fate once they left Egypt and got into the hands of the engravers.

We can now turn from the picturesque descriptions of the adventures of the early visitors to Qurna and take stock of the results obtained by these dedicated travellers turned epigraphists. Although they were naturally interested in mummies and portable antiquities it was, especially to the amateurs Burton and Hay, and to Champollion and Rosellini with all their scholarly background and governmental support, the recording of standing monuments which was their first priority, not excavation as such.

The early publications of scenes from private tombs opened up a whole new world to the lovers of ancient Egypt. The pyramid builders and their descendants became human, and aspects of their civilisation apart from the monumental could now be appreciated. The decipherment of the hieroglyphs by Champollion in 1822 was the key to a better understanding of the ancient people, and the careful epigraphic work made a wealth of texts available to scholars back in Europe.

The ground covered was impressive. Rosellini says that in his days more than three hundred tombs were known. This figure may have included underground mummy-pits. The number of decorated tombs mentioned in the early records, some with ample illustrations, is at least 135. Wilkinson, who stayed for so long in the necropolis, left records of eighty-one decorated tombs; Hay and his party covered fifty-eight; Burton twenty-eight single handed; and Champollion and Rosellini some seventy-five decorated tombs between them. For comparison the present number of decorated tombs, including 'lost' tombs, is about 464.

> 'The present state of the Theban tombs is like that of all the other tombs in Egypt ruined and disorderly [writes Rosellini]. But some still display an amazing freshness in the colours of the pictures . . . Others are completely destroyed, either through fire or because of formations of salt in the folds and creeks of the rock . . . Finally the pictures in many others are deteriorating from one day to the other because having been open for a long time they serve as refuge for Arab families.'

What men have built men will destroy. There was a long way to go before the long-suffering tombs were safeguarded.

Apart from Wilkinson's study and interpretation of the scenes, which is remarkably lucid, it is the illustrations more than the texts of the early publications which have proved to be of lasting value in providing the raw material for further research. For the early records are by no means exhausted. Scenes now damaged can be reconstructed by turning to publications or manuscripts, and entire tombs whose location is no longer known can be built up on paper using the tracings and drawings. With luck, fragments removed by the early travellers can be assigned to their original positions in a tomb which is now to all intents and purposes lost.

This is well illustrated in the case of tombs no. A4 and C4 (tombs in the official list preceded by a letter are those whose exact location is now unknown). Tomb no. A4 has already been referred to above (p. 14). It belonged to Wensu, scribe of the accounts of grain in the reign of Tuthmosis III. It was located at Dra' Abû el-Naga' on the south side of the large valley cutting that part of the necropolis in half, but fairly low down on the slope of the hill, where tombs are particularly prone to destruction and being sanded up. The tomb itself must still be somewhere under the rubble.

Burton has it that the tomb was discovered by Yanni, Salt's agent, around 1821. It had in fact been visited by Hamilton in 1801, and it is amazing that it had not been completely destroyed during the intervening years. But Hay and Burton report extensive damage to the walls in the hall in the attempt to detach pieces of wall-paintings. Nevertheless they found the tomb worth recording, for the inner chamber with funerary scenes, of less interest to the collector, remained intact along with a market scene in the hall. Hay and Burton drew what they could with their *camera lucida* (Wilkinson drew only a few sketches in this tomb). Some of the missing parts of the decoration have been discovered in the Louvre, bought by Champollion from the Salt collection.

Since 1927 the owner of the tomb was believed to be a different individual, and the link with the Louvre fragments, which actually carry Wensu's name and title, was never realised. But the manuscripts of Hay and Burton give the name of the mummy in the funeral ceremonies as Wensu (a very uncommon name), and the connection is indisputable. Thanks to the fact that Hay gave a sketched plan of the tomb and Burton provided the measurements, the task of reconstructing the scheme of decoration was greatly facilitated. Missing portions can be conjectured from stray references. The banquet scene, an ever popular target for collectors, had almost completely vanished and is perhaps still in some private collection. The fishing and fowling scenes, and the hunting in the desert presumably suffered a similar fate. A statue of Wensu, very likely from the tomb, was acquired by a family acquainted with Salt in Cairo. It is now in Leiden. Another statue, this time showing Wensu accompanied by his wife Amenḥotp, came to the Louvre.

The owner of tomb no. C4 was a priest of Ma'et, goddess of Truth, called Meryma'et ('beloved of Ma'et'). The temple to which he was attached must have been the building at Karnak, erected a few years before Meryma'et's time by Amenophis III. The tomb was situated at

Sheikh ʿAbd el-Qurna, 'behind Yanni's house', somewhere up the hill. It was visited by most of the early travellers who drew selected scenes. The greatest help in the reconstruction of this tomb came from a source which we have not yet referred to. Algernon Percy (Lord Prudhoe, 1792–1865) made a career in the navy and travelled in the Middle East. He met Champollion in Nubia in 1828 and made a large collection of antiquities which is now in the University of Durham. A number of drawings were made by Major O. Felix (1790–1860), who accompanied Lord Prudhoe. In tomb no. C4 his sketches of large portions of the walls greatly helped in piecing together the selected subjects drawn by the other artists. But the greatest help was perhaps that the tomb was rediscovered in recent years, a fact unknown to most. In the early 1960s a donkey put its hoof through a hole in the ground below a house which is situated opposite the tomb of Menna (no. 69). An investigation was carried out by the local inspector Mohammed Saleh (now Dr), and he was able to identify the much ruined tomb which appeared as that of Merymaʿet. Nothing was published about the discovery, but in the spring of 1985 the present writer was able to enter the tomb. No decoration of any consequence remained on the walls, but numerous fragments were found lying on the floor of the tomb. These showed the high quality which had been suggested by the drawings of the early travellers as well as by fragments removed in the previous century. Rosellini brought back to Tuscany three fragments of the wall-decoration which are now in Florence. Thanks to the hieroglyphs on these fragments their original provenance has now been ascertained.

FIGURE 85
A fragment of wall decoration from TT C4 emerging from the dust.

The decoration included an elaborate funeral procession and an unusual scene showing funerary rites taking place on a lake, a motif referred to once in a later Theban tomb and once at Memphis. The Feast of the Valley, offering scenes and a representation of Osiris were not omitted, and an interesting inscription declares that the tomb was found locked up by a relative of Merymaʿet, who restored the decoration, presumably after the Amarna period. Traces of this restoration work were found on some of the remaining fragments. So was also a layer of more recent mud plaster which had been applied to the walls just before Hay and Burton visited the tomb. The fact that the physical remains of the tomb were rediscovered greatly facilitated the work of reconstructing the decoration on paper, the dimensions of the walls providing the clue to the position of certain scenes which was otherwise less straightforward to ascertain.

The Ramessid tomb of Kynebu (no. 113) suffered a different fate. Without the drawings made by Wilkinson and Hay the tomb would be of little importance today. Soon after they went there (for neither Champollion nor Rosellini, nor any subsequent traveller left any record of the tomb) a huge boulder came crashing down from the mountain and landed in the hall, destroying the roof and most of the decoration which was by then left in that area. Three fragments of the decoration are now in the British Museum, having been presented to the Museum in 1868 by Hay's son. It would be inconceivable to imagine Hay himself cutting the decoration to pieces. He must either have collected them from the debris after the accident, or someone else did and sold them to him.

The tiny tomb is allegedly inaccessible, but by crawling over a heap of rubble and squeezing past the boulder it was possible in 1985 to get in and inspect the few remaining patches of plaster. It was once a charming little tomb: 'The colours are very fresh and tho' the painting is crude[?] what remains of it is very perfect and satisfactory. It is one of those examples of careless painting for which we may at the same time conclude the artist was no inferior draughtsman,' Hay wrote. His drawings by *camera lucida* and watercolour bear witness to this, as do indeed the three fragments in the British Museum (see also FIGURE 3).

The skill and accuracy displayed by Hay and his party when working with their oiled tracing paper is evident when one compares their work with existing wall-decoration, and it is particularly useful when one is faced with scenes which are now partly destroyed, either through wear and tear or through deliberate destruction. The tomb of Nakht (no. 161),

FIGURE 86
Fragment of wall painting from TT C4, covered with mud plaster in modern times.

FIGURE 87
Drawing by *camera lucida* of a wall in TT 113. Hay MSS 29822, 113.

the gardener, illustrates this very well. Being right among the houses of the village of Draʿ Abû el-Nagaʿ the tomb has suffered a great deal over the past one hundred and sixty years, and fragments were cut from the walls, probably around the turn of the century. Three are now in the Ny Carlsberg Glyptotek in Copenhagen, whereas a fourth found its way to the Musée Rodin in Paris. Hay left a complete record of the texts in the tomb – although he had no intimate knowledge of the language there are very few errors in his copies – as well as watercolours and tracings of scenes which are now in a poor state. The craftsmanship of the original paintings is well captured by Hay, and his tracings have provided the basis for line drawings of acceptable quality.

During the years following the departure of the Franco-Italian expedition little scientific work seems to have been undertaken in the tombs. But the French architect and engineer Prisse d'Avennes (1807–79), who was employed by Mohammed Ali, became interested in the monuments. He made numerous drawings, published in 1857–77 and as a history of Egyptian art in 1878. Prisse had entered and copied scenes in thirteen of the private tombs, and where subjects are now destroyed, his records are a valuable contribution.

The season 1844–45 saw the last expedition on a grand scale at Thebes, this time sent by the King of Prussia, who had acquired the collection of Passalacqua some twenty years before. It was headed by R. Lepsius (1810–84), one of the greatest names in the history of Egyptology. He had prepared himself well for the task by visiting all major collections

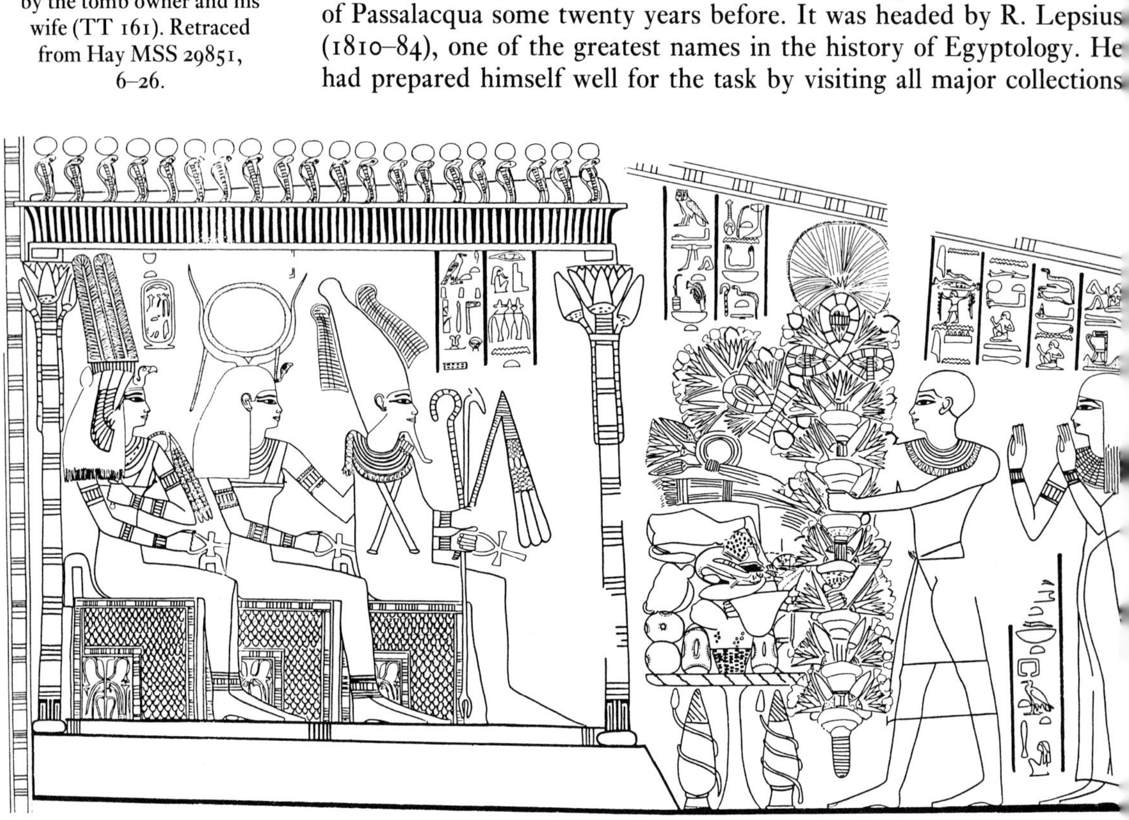

FIGURE 88
Queen ʿAḥmosi Nefertere, Ḥatḥor and Osiris adored by the tomb owner and his wife (TT 161). Retraced from Hay MSS 29851, 6–26.

in Europe, and he assembled an expert team. The purpose of the expedition was to record monuments and collect antiquities, and they completed both in style. 15,000 pieces were officially presented by Mohammed Ali to the King of Prussia. The epigraphic results were published in twelve mammoth volumes in 1849–59, the text volumes being compiled after Lepsius' death, appearing in five volumes in 1897–1913.

The expedition spent almost five months staying at Thebes in Wilkinson's house and recording tombs and temples. The private tombs were not neglected. 110 decorated tombs were visited and some copied in great detail. Thirty-five had not been recorded by earlier travellers. Among them was the tomb of Antefoḳer (no. 60), the large Middle Kingdom tomb near the summit of Sheikh ʿAbd el-Qurna, though for some reason only a short text was copied in this interesting tomb of a period so sparingly represented in the necropolis. The same was the case with the tomb of Sebkḥotp (no. 63), a mayor in the reign of Tuthmosis IV. The decoration of this splendid tomb is now cut to pieces and scattered in various collections, including the British Museum. One of the fragments was acquired by the Museum in 1852 from J. W. Wild who was actually a member of Lepsius' expedition; four others came to the museum in 1869. Some fragments have now been replaced on the walls, while others are to this day lying around on the floor.

A number of the tombs seen by the expedition have now vanished, and the sole proof of their existence are brief entries in Lepsius' unpublished notebook. Evidence for another tomb also relies chiefly on Lepsius' notes, although a few texts were copied by earlier travellers. Tomb no. C6 belonged to Ipy, overseer of boats in the mortuary temple of Tuthmosis IV. No one copied the scenes in this tomb, in spite of the fact that the paintings were said to be 'very neat' and 'covered by a brilliant varnish'. In Lepsius' notebook the inscriptions are copied with the hieroglyphs in their original position. The direction of the signs always bears a definite relation to the direction of the figures to which the signs appertain. Assisted by the comments in Lepsius' difficult handwriting it is possible to a certain extent to reconstruct the scheme of

FIGURE 89
A detail from TT 161 in its present state.

FIGURE 91
TT 77: the wall in its present state.

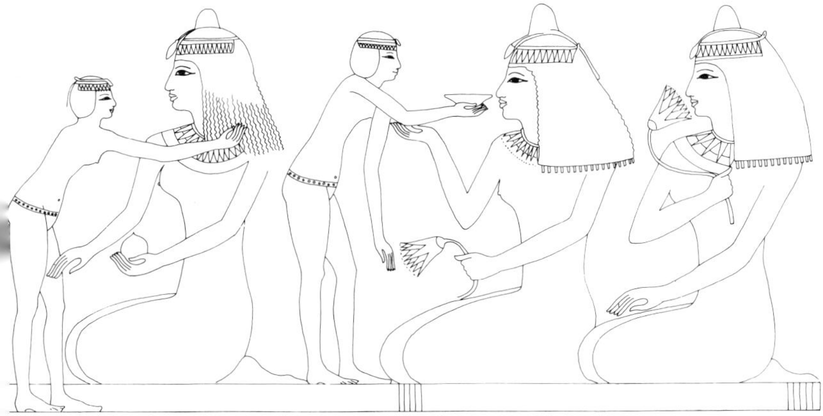

FIGURE 90
Drawing by Prisse d'Avennes of banqueting ladies in TT 77.

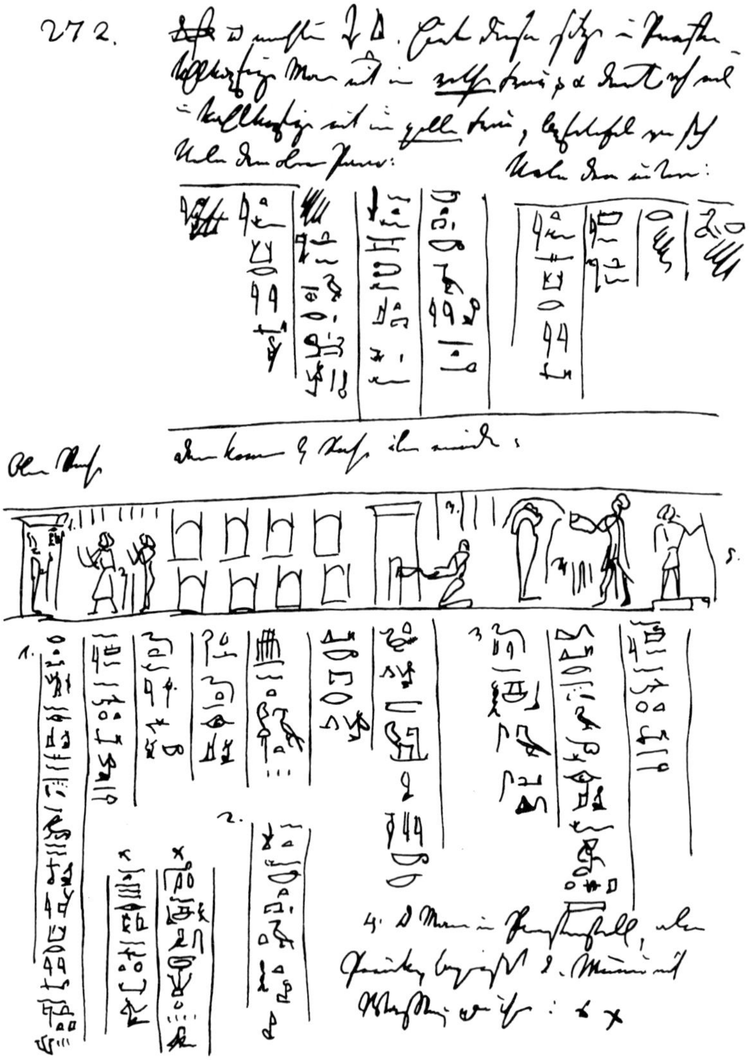

FIGURE 92
A page of Lepsius' notebook referring to TT 161.

decoration. We are left guessing as to the style and quality of the work, but without Lepsius' observations we would have little more than a handful of names and titles.

In one of the tombs at Deir el-Medîna the expedition managed to detach two large pieces of plaster showing the deified King Amenophis I and his mother, Queen ʿAḥmosi Nefertere, patrons of the necropolis. These operations were apparently carried out quite openly, and the paintings were included in the package given away by Mohammed Ali.

7
MODERN TIMES

A proposed visit to the necropolis by a cousin of Napoleon III, also called Napoleon, was instrumental in the creation of the Egyptian Antiquities Service in 1858. The French scholar A. Mariette (1821–81) had been sent to Egypt to acquire manuscripts for the Louvre, but instead he began excavations which led to the discovery of the burials of the Apis bulls at the Serapeum in Saqqâra. When the distinguished French visitor had announced his arrival, the Khedive (viceroy of Egypt) entrusted Mariette with the task of digging for antiquities which could then be re-buried and re-excavated in the presence of the Prince. Mariette dug his spade into ground north of the crossroads which lead from the river to the Valley of the Kings and from north to south along the mountain. The Prince never arrived, but Mariette thus discovered the tombs of the kings of the Seventeenth dynasty. A choice of objects found were presented to the Prince, and he in turn saw to it that Mariette was made Director of Antiquities. The Antiquities Service had come into being. Although for many years in the future Europeans were to hold the key positions in the organisation, the awareness of the Egyptians of their past and its monuments had been awakened.

In the three decades after Lepsius' departure (1845) the necropolis was again a field of research for private individuals. Mariette, digging on behalf of the Egyptians, stumbled on royal burials, but the area he explored is part of the necropolis of Qurna.

In 1856–7 extensive excavations were carried out all over the necropolis, as well as in the Valley of the Kings, by a man whose career was to have been in a totally different field. Ill-health introduced a number of people to Egypt, including A.H. Rhind (1833–63). He was a Scot-

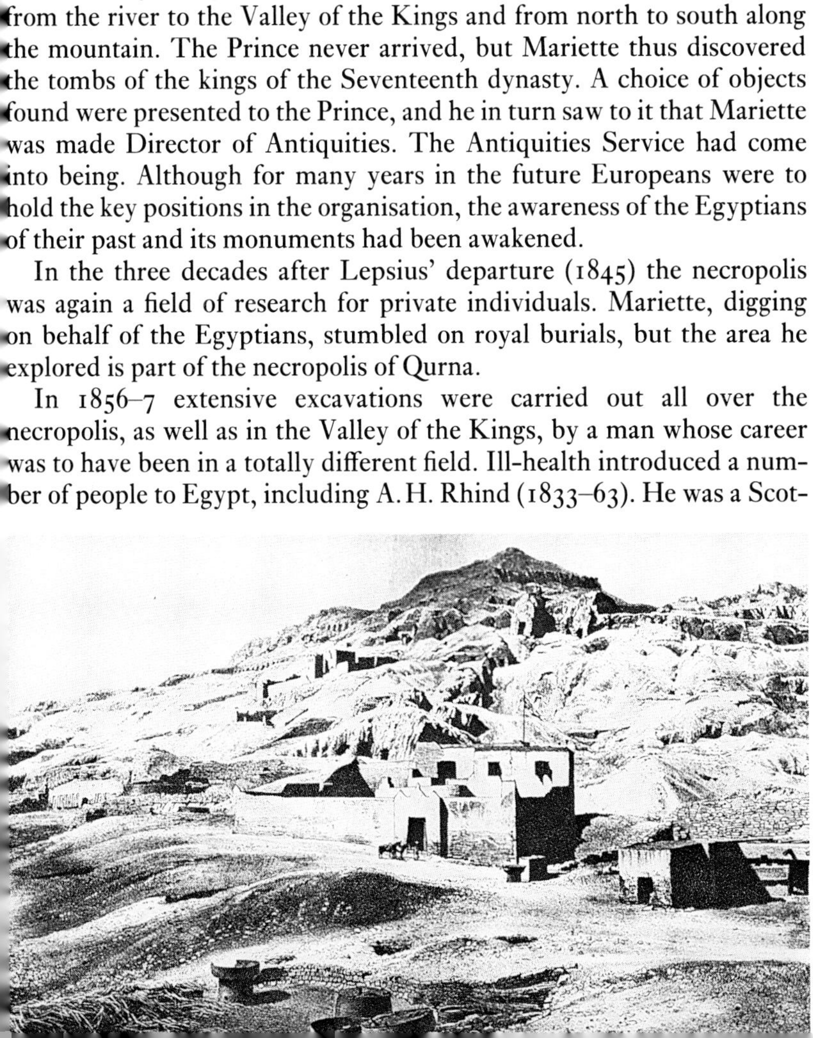

FIGURE 93
The Theban necropolis as published by Rhind on the basis of an early photograph. The English diplomat H. Salt used to live in the large house in the foreground. The towers on the hill are part of Wilkinson's residence, later also used by Lepsius.

tish lawyer of private means who came to spend the winter in Egypt. He immediately saw what had to be done. He was outraged at the way in which previous excavators had ravaged the tombs without leaving any records of the circumstances of their finds and their provenance. His book *Thebes. Its Tombs and their Tenants* from 1862 is not an excavation report as we understand it today, but nevertheless it gives more details of his excavations, including the abortive ones, than any previous book had done. Apart from an intact Roman burial in a re-used tomb (see above, pp. 91–2), his finds were not even very spectacular, but his comments are sensible and objective. Separate chapters deal with the inhabitants of the tombs in the 1850s, their daily life and its problems which Rhind had an opportunity to observe from his residence in Salt's old house at Sheikh ʿAbd el-Qurna. As a matter of interest it should be noted that a photograph was used as a basis for one of the plates in his book. Rhind's collection of antiquities are now mostly in the Royal Museum of Scotland in Edinburgh, and two important papyri bear his name. His publication on the necropolis was a major step forward, and his indefatigable struggle to preserve the monuments intact instead of tearing them to pieces (he refers to what Lepsius had done just a few years before) is admirable.

In the 1880s French scholars began to undertake the publication of the first monographs on private tombs. Unfortunately their epigraphic skills were never up to the standards of their predecessors, and most of the drawings, some of which are in colour, have the appearance of handcopies. The tomb of Rekhmirēʿ (no. 100) received its first publication in this fashion.

It was during these years that the tomb of Nakht (no. 52) was discovered. Along with the tomb of Raʿmosi, discovered in 1860 it has for a long time been a must on the tourist's itinerary. Travellers a hundred years ago might have the good fortune of bringing back as a souvenir an actual fragment of a tomb. It must have been around this time that a visitor acquired four tiny fragments of decorated plaster which undoubtedly came from the very tomb of Nakht. For the past fifteen years it has been on loan to The Brooklyn Museum, having previously been kept in a school. At the time the tomb was discovered fragments of plaster were already lying on the floor, and it was all too easy for someone to pick them up and dispose of them to a tourist. Larger fragments of painted plaster were bought in 1885 by a German traveller who presented them to the museum in Dresden. They stem from a tomb of the Eighteenth dynasty, and due to the fact that very few tombs of this date show the yellow background colour of the fragments, they can tentatively be assigned to the tomb of Ḳenamūn (no. 93), a tomb already known to the early travellers.

A systematic clearance of a large area of Draʿ Abû el-Nagaʿ was undertaken in 1898–9 by an expedition funded by the 5th Marquis of Northampton and headed by W. Spiegelberg (1870–1930) of the University of Strasbourg, and P.E. Newberry (1869–1949), who was in the process

FIGURE 94
Four tiny fragments from the tomb of Nakht (TT 52), on loan to The Brooklyn Museum. Courtesy of The Brooklyn Museum.

of carrying out a survey of the necropolis. Between forty and eighty men were at work every day for four and a half months. A number of royal monuments were discovered, as well as an ibis and hawk cemetery of the second century BC. Seven private tombs were cleared, including one mentioned in the records of the great tomb robberies which took place during the Twentieth dynasty: at the foot of the pyramid of the tomb of King Sebkemsaf of the Thirteenth dynasty, which the team had just found, they came across the tomb of Nebamūn, an official in the granary of Tuthmosis III (no. 149), the very tomb mentioned in the papyrus records as being that through which the robbers forced their way into the tomb of King Sebkemsaf. The excavators even found the passage leading from the tomb of Nebamūn into the royal monument.

Somewhere in the area, between tomb no. 14 and 165, the expedition recovered a small fragment of painted plaster showing four men catching quail. The fragment eventually ended up in the Rustafjaell collection (see below), and was later acquired by the Berlin Museum. It was this little painting which inspired the present writer to return to the spot where Spiegelberg and Newberry had dug and investigate to see if the site could possibly still hold the clue to a long-standing mystery: the provenance of the eleven beautiful wall-paintings in the British Museum (see above, p. 61).

Sir W. M. F. Petrie (1853–1942), who excavated so many sites in Egypt during his long life, spent two months at Thebes in 1908–9. Among

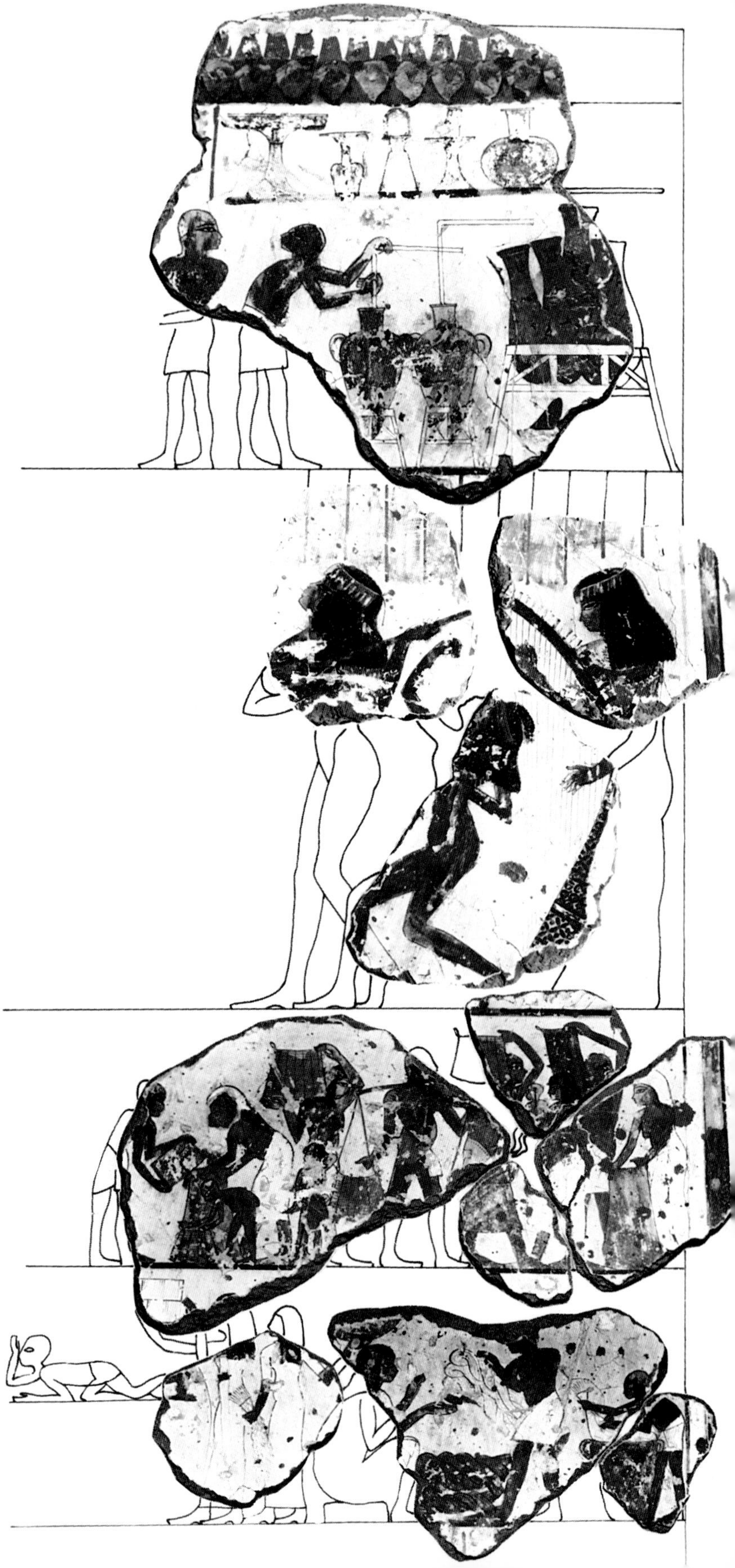

FIGURE 95
Fragments of a wall of a tomb now in the Museo Egizio, Turin, showing bottling wine, musicians, harvest, and laundry. Courtesy of the Museo Egizion, Turin.

his finds were the meagre fragments of wall-paintings from a tomb of the Seventeenth dynasty showing rows of dancers. Due to the impossibility of protecting them on the site, they were removed and are now in the Ashmolean Museum in Oxford. Petrie discovered two more painted tombs, and an interesting unopened burial also of the Seventeenth dynasty. His excavation report appeared with his usual promptness the following year. It included numerous drawings of pots and other smaller objects recovered from the site, so often neglected by previous excavators.

H. Carter (1874–1939), whose name is chiefly connected with the discovery of the Tomb of Tutʿankhamūn, had been Inspector General of Upper Egypt from 1899–1903, and in the years between 1907 and 1911 he carried out extensive work in the necropolis on behalf of Lord Carnavon. Both royal and private tombs were discovered during this period, and Carter's skill as a draughtsman resulted in excellent copies of wall-paintings.

With the excavations of E. Schiaparelli (1856–1928) in 1905 and following years attention is once more focused on Deir el-Medîna. After the discovery of the tomb of Sennezem (no. 1) in 1886 (see above, pp. 80–1) the necropolis yielded another unrifled burial, the tomb of Khaʿ (no. 8), the architect, and his wife Meryt. This time an adequate report was made, although it took almost twenty years to have it published. The finds from the tomb are now among the main attractions of the Egyptian Museum in Turin, revealing a wealth of details of daily life towards the end of the Eighteenth dynasty (see above, p. 47). The wall-paintings in the upper chapel were left *in situ*. But the neighbouring chapel, the tomb (no. 138) of Maya, the draughtsman, was dismantled in 1906 and rebuilt in the Museum.

Prior to his excavations at Deir el-Medîna Schiaparelli had acquired a number of fragments of wall-paintings from tombs at Deir el-Medîna as well as from other parts of the necropolis. A group of twelve fragments is particularly interesting because they can be joined together to form one small and one large section of a wall. At present they are exhibited separately in horizontal glass cases, though grouped according to subject.

The tomb from which the fragments came is unknown. But if the decoration included a weaving scene, as the dyed or bleached yarn may suggest, it may have belonged in one of the very few tombs of weavers in the necropolis. One such, of a suitable date, is the tomb of Senenrēʿ (no. 246). This tomb is now inaccessible, being filled with rubble, but early in the century it was found that fragments had been removed through an entrance made from a neighbouring house. It would be gratifying one day to be able to assign a certain provenance to these interesting paintings.

The same can be said of a very large collection of mostly very small fragments which were on the market around the same time. They were bought by R. de Rustafjaell (d. 1943), an American travelling in Egypt who was chiefly interested in prehistory. He disposed of most of his collection soon after at Sotheby's in London in 1906, 1907 and 1910, and in New York in 1915. The paintings are now scattered in numerous collections, many in provincial museums in England, having been bought for the Wellcome collection. But others can no longer be traced. The sale catalogues were only partly illustrated and the descriptions quite inadequate. A few were fakes or restored beyond recognition, and all but a fraction remain unidentified. As they are by no means choice pieces and of limited artistic value, only a proper context makes them worthy of interest. The exceptions are a few of those acquired by the Berlin Museum of which we had occasion to speak above.

It was by now painfully obvious that some adequate protection of the tombs had to be devised. When A. Weigall (1880–1934) became Inspector General of Upper Egypt in 1905 he immediately set about it. In 1903 only eight tombs had iron doors, put up by Carter, his predecessor in office. In 1902–7 R. Mond (1867–1938), later knighted, an English chemist, undertook extensive excavations and restorations in the necropolis at his own expense. Numerous tombs and pits were excavated, tombs and courtyards cleared, walls cleaned, iron doors installed and reports written. When Mond was unable to carry out the work in person he sent out a replacement, E. Mackay (1880–1943) who became responsible for the campaign which lasted until 1916 and was resumed after the war with W.B. Emery (1903–71) taking an active part in the work of restoration. The work included expropriation of families living in the tombs; conservation work and safe-guarding; replacement of missing portions of reliefs now in museums with casts; and last but not least a complete photographic survey of as many tombs as possible.

To this end Mond had designed a cast-iron carriage for his camera, carrying a steel tubular mast on which the camera could be moved up or down. The carriage ran on smooth rails and easily moved sideways as well. Light was provided by a set of incandescent lamps attached to the camera lamp and powered by a portable motor-dynamo. In this way a whole wall could be photographed to give the complete picture. The

FIGURE 96
A wall in TT 81 of Ineni showing a list of offerings presented to the tomb owner and his wife, photographed in sections, assembled and re-photographed by Mond. Courtesy of the Griffith Institute, Oxford.

glass plates were developed in the excavation house which Mond had built on the mountain. Hot though it seemed, an ingenious yet simple method was devised to keep the room cool before the days of air-conditioning: the room had a door at one end and a window at the other. A second room was built inside with the door at the opposite end to the first, and with a small chimney. The outer chamber was provided with a tunnel containing three large porous water jars. With a constant draught of air circulating past the pots, round the inner chamber and up through the chimney, the room was kept reasonably cool. Fifteen tombs were completely recorded with Mond's equipment, and numerous photos were taken in other tombs. These photographic archives are now available for consultation in the Griffith Institute in Oxford. Mond also carried out research into colour photography of colour facsimiles of tomb paintings, and for many years to come his work set the standard for this kind of recording in the tombs.

By 1908 the tombs were beginning to be in some sort of order. Doors had been fitted, either of wood, or iron grilles with wire netting, to keep out the bats. Weigall had the clever idea of involving officials on the spot in the safeguarding, and a number of people contributed to doors and restorations. Connecting paths among the tombs were made, and a reinforced stone wall was built around a large group of tombs at Sheikh ʿAbd el-Qurna to keep intruders away. The cost of the 1200 m of wall, £50 sterling, was met by Mond. A *gafir*, or guard, was installed in each section of the necropolis, and all these precautions appear to have kept tomb robbers and vandals at bay for a while.

A final numbering system of the tombs was worked out, based on a list made by Newberry. When in 1913 the *Topographical Catalogue of the Private Tombs at Thebes* was published, 252 tombs were included. Out of these 161 were now well protected. The supplement of 1924 took the number of tombs to 334. A wooden board with the tomb number was nailed outside the entrance to the tomb, and inside was placed a framed notice giving the owner's name and title, the date of the tomb, the date of restoration work and the name of the person at whose expense the repairs had been carried out.

Weigall's duties as Inspector General involved him with the inhabitants of Qurna in many ways, his tasks most often being of an unpleasant nature. Expropriating families and always being engaged in tearing down the walls they built up to extend their territory over land owned by the Antiquities Service cannot have made him a popular man. In his first year as Inspector he had to make a report of a strange incident in one of the tombs on the hillside of Draʿ Abû el-Nagaʿ, just north of the temple of Deir el-Baḥri. The undecorated tomb was used by a family as a stable and lumber-room. One day, on removing some rubbish from his cave, the owner discovered an entrance to a passage descending into the rock. Each day he dug away a portion of the stones blocking the doorway, hoping to find innumerable treasures at the other end. His family was told, but he chose a day when they were away to force his way through the hole. The following morning his wife became anxious about his disappearance and went through the passage in search of him. She was in turn followed by her mother and a cousin, and yet another cousin. When an hour had passed and no one had returned, two of the people who had gathered at the entrance decided to enter with candles. Three yards beyond the entrance the passage turned sharply to the left, then to the left again. Here the candles began to fail, but a moment later they came across the second cousin lying on floor. They dragged him out, but he soon expired. The police then arrived with an antiquities inspector. This latter and four others entered the passage and found that beyond the spot where the body had been found the passage turned right, then left again and opened into a hall with four rough columns. The air was foul, and the candles began to go out, but they think that they caught a glimpse of the three bodies. They were unable to reach them, being overcome with nausea. On their return no one dared enter again, for the general opinion was that an *afrit*, an evil spirit, had overpowered the victims. The following day the passage was blocked up, the bodies left where they had fallen. The cause of death was registered as asphyxia produced by poisonous gases. When Weigall visited the place a few days later, the house and cave had been taken over by the next door neighbours, and there was not a single sign of the tragedy remaining.

While Mond and his staff were excavating and restoring, and Weigall was counting tombs, another expedition had established itself at Qurna. The Graphic Section of the Egyptian Expedition of the Metropolitan Museum of Art in New York, headed by the English clergyman, archaeologist and draughtsman N. de Garis Davies (1865–1941) had arrived and in the season of 1907–8 began to record the tombs in facsimiles, drawings and photographs. Funds for the work and, equally important, its publication were provided by Mrs C. M. Tytus in memory of her son Robb de Peyster Tytus. The team included Davies' wife, Nina M. de Garis Davies (1881–1965) who was even more skilled than her husband when it came to doing facsimiles in colour.

In the previous century Hay and his team had worked in watercolour which, being by nature transparent, was not ideally suited for imitating the quality of the ancient pigments. It was discovered that tempera bound with egg was much more satisfactory. The first step in the proceedings was to make a tracing of the scene to be painted. This was done by candlelight which seemed to penetrate the tracing paper better than the intricate system of mirrors catching the rays of the sun otherwise in use. By means of graphite paper the tracings were transferred to watercolour paper, having previously been reduced to a more manageable size. If the drawing was to be black and white, the scene was inked in on the tracing paper.

Before the Egyptian Expedition came to an end in 1936 the members had produced no less than 365 painted facsimiles, a great number of which are now on display in the galleries of the Metropolitan Museum. Davies published a substantial number of tombs, either on his own or with his wife, partly for the lavish folio editions of the Metropolitan Museum, partly for the more modest, but equally useful series published by the Egypt Exploration Fund (later Society), which had been created back in England in 1882. The line-drawings are unsurpassed in quality. Where scenes were damaged Davies often had recourse to drawings done by Hay in the previous century. The photographic work was carried out by the American H. Burton (1879–1940) who later made his name in the Valley of the Kings when in 1922 Carter discovered the tomb of Tutʿankhamūn.

From 1910 the field director of the Egyptian Expedition was H.E. Winlock (1884–1950). It was during his work at the temples at Deir el-Baḥri in 1920 that he stumbled on a find of extraordinary interest, though the treasures of Tutʿankhamūn were to catch the limelight shortly afterwards.

The tomb of Meketrēʿ, chancellor of the king during the Eleventh dynasty (see above, p. 21) had been known since the beginning of the century, but its decoration was reduced to fragments. Winlock and his team had worked for three weeks hoping to find more pieces in the debris on the floor. Some ancient quarrymen had smashed up the façade of the tomb to get stone for their own buildings. Their hammers and rollers were found under a pile of rubbish where the excavators had pinned their last hopes of finding something interesting. All that was then left to do was to clear some fallen stones, make a plan, and leave.

It was 17 March, and it would soon have been too uncomfortable to work in this the hottest part of the necropolis. Winlock was riding back to the excavation house on his donkey while the sun was setting behind the mountain. He was contemplating his bad luck that season when he overtook one of his workmen, who insisted on saluting him.

> '"I am going home," he informed me [wrote Winlock], and I said that that seemed evident. "And when I get my blankets I am going back to spend the night at the tomb." For the life of me I couldn't remember whether we kept guards up there at night to look after the equipment, but I supposed we must, and as I started on again I laughingly hoped that he had something to watch. "The headman Hamid says I must tell no one, but your Honor will see something up there," Abdullahi called after me.
>
> He had charged his voice with all the mysteriousness he could put into it and his whole manner would have been strange enough to impress me at any other time, but I was convinced of failure, and when I remembered that Abdullahi belonged to one of the gangs which were clearing those corridors, I knew perfectly well there could be nothing to it all.
>
> At the house I met Lansing [a curator of the Museum] and our associate Walter Hauser coming out. They said they were going up to the work, and showed me a scrap of paper with a hastily scribbled note from Burton: "Come *at once* and bring your electric torch. Good luck *at last*." This seemed preposterous. Surely it was another false alarm, and we had had so many of them. However, there was Abdullahi and his mysteriousness, and I decided

FIGURE 97
The hidden room in the tomb of Meketrē' as discovered by Winlock. Courtesy of The Metropolitan Museum of Art. Photography by Egyptian Expedition of The Metropolitan Museum of Art.

to let my tea wait a while and go along with them, but I refused to have any hopes, and the three of us got ready all sorts of sarcasms for Burton's benefit as we trudged along. A little knot of Egyptians were standing around the mouth of the tomb in the twilight. Inside in the gloom we could just make out Burton and the head men. There was something in the air which made our sarcasms sound flat. Burton pointed to a yawning black crack between the wall of the corridor and the rock floor. He said he had tried to look in with matches but they didn't give light enough and told us to try the torches.

At least a hole there was unexpected, but we had looked into so many empty holes. Anyway, I got down flat on my stomach, pushed the torch into the hole, pressed the button, and looked in.

The beam of light shot into a little world of four thousand years ago, and I was gazing down into the midst of a myriad of brightly painted little men going this way and that. A tall, slender girl gazed across at me perfectly composed; a gang of little men with sticks in their upraised hands drove spotted oxen; rowers tugged at their oars on a fleet of boats, while one ship seemed foundering right in front of me with its bow balanced precariously in the air. And all of this busy coming and going was in uncanny silence, as though the distance back over the forty centuries I looked across was too great for even an echo to reach my ears.'

Winlock had discovered a cache of tomb models showing like dolls' houses all the activities on a large estate around 2000 BC. This breathtaking find was later divided between the Egyptian Museum in Cairo and the Metropolitan Museum of Art in New York.

As if this were not enough for one season, soon afterwards the team found the unspoilt burial of Meketrē''s butler, Waḥ, who had been laid to rest in a small tomb below that of his master (see above, pp. 22–3).

In the season of 1921–3 the University Museum, Philadelphia was engaged in studying a number of Ramessid tombs at Dra' Abû el-Naga'. Although the photographic records are available to scholars, the results of the work have never been published. But at the opposite end of the necropolis the French were about to enter on a large scale project to clear the tombs and houses at Deir el-Medîna from top to bottom. Under the inspired directorship of B. Bruyère (1879–1971) the *Institut français d'archéologie orientale* settled down in a house on the hillside in 1922 where they remained until 1953, the work being occasionally resumed to this day. For the first time it was possible to gain an insight into the daily life of a group of Egyptian workmen beyond the facts which had previously been gleaned from tomb paintings and similar sources. Tombs and houses were thoroughly excavated and cleared and yielded not only numerous artefacts but also thousands of ostraka: flakes of limestone or potsherds with sketches or texts. All these documents, a great many of which have been published, throw light on a wealth of details of the daily life of the inhabitants who in addition had an interesting occupation: they were pharaoh's tomb builders.

With all these activities going on at Qurna and in the whole area of Thebes, the need for a proper map was evident. Wilkinson had already embarked on the project and published his *Topographical Survey of Thebes* in 1830. Major monuments were indicated, but only a selection of tombs. Both Burton and a member of Hay's party had drawn maps, and Lepsius published his version in 1849. But the private tombs were sadly neglected. In 1921 a complete survey had been carried out and the area mapped out on thirty-six sheets at 1 : 1000. R. Engelbach (1888–1946) had taken over the Inspectorate of Upper Egypt the year before, and through the Survey Department it was he who was in charge of bringing previous maps up to date, inserting new tombs as well as the houses which kept changing as the inhabitants encroached upon the land. This useful working tool will in the near future be superseded by another map, currently being prepared at the University of California at Berkeley, using all modern technology.

The year 1927 saw the publication of a book without which the Egyptologist at his desk would hardly be able to work: the *Topographical Bibliography of Ancient Egyptian Hieroglyphic Texts, Reliefs, and Paintings*, I, *The Theban Necropolis*, the first in a series eventually covering all sites in Egypt and Egyptian material from neighbouring countries. Each tomb is here listed in numerical order, with a plan and its location on a map, including a brief description of all the scenes on the walls with bibliographical references. The work was carried out by Miss B. Porter (1852–1941), assisted by Miss R.L.B. Moss, who produced the subsequent volumes. The entry slips, housed in the Griffith Institute in Oxford, are being kept up to date, and revised editions, now supervised by Dr J. Málek, are being prepared. The second edition of vol. 1, appearing in two parts separating the private and the royal tombs, of 1960 and 1964 respectively, is already out of date, but a third edition will not be available for many years to come.

For the Egyptologist in the field who wanted to check references in the midst of the desert (or very nearly) the Oriental Institute of Chicago soon provided excellent facilities. Across the river in Luxor Chicago

House sprang up in 1930, endowed with a magnificent library and accommodation for the staff who were embarking on the herculean task of recording the temple of Medînet Habu. Simultaneously a great many photographs were taken all over the necropolis, though only one tomb (no. 192), that of Kharuef, steward of Queen Teye, has been published till now.

The draughtsmen of the Oriental Institute used a drawing technique which had already been tried out by Carter many years before. The monuments copied were mostly in relief. The scenes were photographed and large prints made. The draughtsman now drew directly on the photograph with permanent ink. By immersing the photograph in an iodine solution the photograph disappeared, but the line-drawing remained. A number of different artists were at work over the years, but the drawings are surprisingly uniform in character, checked and double-checked, and beautifully printed.

Working in collaboration with the Oriental Institute S. Schott dedicated a substantial part of his time to the Theban tombs. His photographic records are comprehensive and of high quality, often with interesting details used as illustrations in his publications of other subjects. He made a particular study of Theban feasts, and especially the Feast of the Valley celebrated annually in and around the tombs.

Before World War II closed down excavations in Egypt, a number of tombs had been published by French scholars, notably G. Foucart (1865–1946) and E. Drioton (1889–1961). The French school of drawing differed from that of the English and American in that larger areas were inked in in black where the Davies and the Oriental Institute artist preferred to leave the outline (except perhaps for eyes, hair and certain patterns). The general appearance of the drawings is very different, but it is largely a matter of taste which style you prefer.

In 1942 the Inspectorate of Upper Egypt had been taken over by an Egyptian, Dr Ahmed Fakhry (1905–73). During his term of office he had to deal with a number of problems in the tombs. In the years 1937–42 they were subjected to plunder and vandalism, partly because of the absence of many foreign missions to keep an eye on them during the war. The brief reports in the journal of the Antiquities Service hardly do justice to the scale of the destruction. This began in the summer of 1937, and when the state of affairs was pointed out by Davies, some publicity arose, but no effective measures could be taken. L. Keimer (1893–1957), whose specialist subjects were connected with natural history, but who also had a keen interest in Theban tombs, photographed a number of fragments which had appeared on the market in Cairo. By his death in 1957 only a few of the photographs had been published, and the remaining ones are apparently not to be found among his papers. Eventually an inquiry was held, and the Antiquities Service took steps to prevent a similar disaster happening again. More expropriations were envisaged; an inspector was required to live on the spot at Qurna; and long overdue restoration was carried out with a varying degree of success.

FIGURE 98
Fragments of mourners from TT 181 now in the Museum of Fine Arts in Boston.

The full details of the spoliations of forty-two tombs or more have never been disclosed, and the report by the local inspector who undertook the investigations has never been published. Fakhry, who was assisting in the proceedings, wrote a summary account which makes heartbreaking reading. The thieves were clever at masking the damage by imitating the technique of restoration used by Mackay and others, so that in case a tomb had not been published, the extent of the damage was impossible to gauge. Fakhry was able to trace a few of the fragments. Several others have recently been identified by the present writer. As an example we may look at the tomb of Nebamūn and Ipuky (no. 181), sculptors in the reigns of Amenophis III and IV, who had joined forces to make a family tomb (see above, p. 57). Not unexpectedly they chose the best artist to do the paintings – perhaps they sculpted the painter's funerary statues in return? The tomb was published in 1925 by the Davies's. The excellent line-drawings and colour facsimiles make it very easy to identify the fragments later removed. It was not until the 1960s and 1970s that most of the pieces appeared on the art markets of Europe. Eleven fragments are now known to be in collections in Europe and the USA. The tomb is scarred for ever.

FIGURE 99
Attempt at cutting out a fragment in TT 82.

One positive thing which came of the investigations in the necropolis was the re-discovery of part of the tomb of Kharuef (no. 192) mentioned above. The thieves had not bothered to go below the debris, and reliefs of the finest quality were saved for posterity.

It was by now abundantly clear that the people who lived among the tombs would have to go. The more there were, the greater the risk of clandestine entrance and disfiguration of the tomb paintings. In 1943 a council of ministers set aside the sum of £E50,000 for expropriation purposes. The Survey Department began their preliminary work, and the people of Qurna seemed to have accepted their fate. They would

FIGURE 101
The village of New Qurna.

not have far to go, for a site was chosen to the east of the colossi of Memnon, close to the fields. The removal of the people from the tombs was carried out successfully. But the new village, so brilliant on the architect's drawing board, was a failure. Hassan Fathy had designed the perfect village with great sensitivity and with his now widely recognised skill for using local natural materials in his buildings, which were both of great beauty and of the utmost utility. The inhabitants, however, were not prepared to play the part. The village is now as lifeless as the neighbouring temples, and the houses do not in any way fulfil their original purposes.

The past twenty-five years have seen renewed scholarly activity in the necropolis. Outstanding among the publications of tombs are those produced by the German Archaeological Institute, contributing authors being not only German Egyptologists, but also Egyptian, Swiss and Italian scholars. These works emphasise the importance of photography,

FIGURE 100
The author working in TT 100 in 1978.

colour as well as black and white. Colour photography had already been taken to a high standard of perfection by A. Mekhitarian, whose volume *Egyptian Painting* largely draws on paintings from Theban tombs.

In the early 1960s T. Säve-Söderbergh followed in the footsteps of the Davies's by publishing a number of tombs in line-drawings based on records by Nina and Norman de Garis Davies in the Griffith Institute in Oxford. The promising series of tomb publications was discontinued but similar work is now being carried out by N. and H. Strudwick in Cambridge.

In the framework of the *Institut français d'archéologie orientale* have appeared above all works on the tombs of Deir El-Medîna and their owners. But apart from publications of individual tombs studies of subjects related to other tombs in the necropolis are few and far between. In 1935 Marcelle Baud published her important collection of sketches and unfinished drawings copied from a great many tombs. The following year appeared the first short, but comprehensive study of the tombs by G. Steindorff and W. Wolf. The stelae in the tombs were the subject of a dissertation undertaken by A. Hermann during these years. The 'lost' tombs were recently studied for a similar exercise by the present writer. A thorough study of the necropolis as a whole remains to be undertaken, but it is hoped that the present work will have gone some way to fill the gap.

FIGURE 102
The sun resting in the horizon, represented by two lions (TT A16). From Hay MSS 29851, 102.

BIBLIOGRAPHY

ON THEBES IN GENERAL:

J. Capart & M. Werbrouck, *Thebes*. London 1926.
C.F. Nims, *Thebes of the Pharaohs*. London/Toronto 1965.

ON THE THEBAN TOMBS IN PARTICULAR:

B. Porter & R.L.B. Moss, *Topographical Bibliography of Ancient Egyptian Hieroglyphic Texts, Reliefs and Paintings*. I². The Theban Necropolis. Part 1. Private Tombs. Oxford 1960. Part 2. Royal Tombs and Smaller Cemeteries. Oxford 1964.
G. Steindorff & W. Wolf, *Die Thebanische Gräberwelt*. Glückstadt/Hamburg 1936.
A. Mekhitarian, *Egyptian Painting*. Geneva 1954, rp. 1978.
M. Baud, *Les dessins ébauchés de la nécropole thébaine*. (*Mémoires de l'Institut français d'archéologie orientale* lxiii). Cairo 1935.
C.K. Wilkinson with M. Hill, *Egyptian Wall Paintings. The Metropolitan Museum of Art's Collection of Facsimiles*. Metropolitan Museum of Art 1983.
M. Abdul-Qader Muhammed, *The Development of the Funerary Beliefs and Practises Displayed in the Private Tombs of the New Kingdom at Thebes*. Cairo 1966.

ON DEIR EL-MEDÎNA:

M. Bierbrier, *The Tomb-Builders of the Pharaohs*. London 1982.
J. Romer, *Ancient Lives. The Story of the Pharaoh's Tombmakers*. London 1984.

LIST OF THEBAN TOMBS AND THEIR OWNERS

1. **SENNEZEM.** Servant in the Place of Truth. Dyn. XIX.
2. **KHAʿBEKHNET.** Servant in the Place of Truth. Temp. Ramesses II.
3. **PESHEDU.** Servant in the Place of Truth. Ramessid.
4. **ḲEN.** Chiseller of Amūn in the Place of Truth. Temp. Ramesses II.
5. **NEFERʿABET.** Servant in the Place of Truth. Ramessid.
6. **NEFERḤŌTEP and son NEBNŪFER.** Foremen in the Place of Truth. Temp. Ḥaremḥab to Ramesses II.
7. **RAʿMOSI.** Scribe in the Place of Truth. Temp. Ramesses II.
8. **KHAʿ.** Chief in the Great Place. Temp. Amenophis II-III.
9. **AMENMOSI.** Servant in the Place of Truth, Charmer of Scorpions. Ramessid.
10. **PENBUY and KASA.** Servants in the Place of Truth. Temp. Ramesses II.
11. **D̲ḤOUT.** Overseer of the treasury, Overseer of works. Temp. Ḥatshepsut.
12. **ḤRAY.** Overseer of the Granary of the King's wife and King's mother ʿAḥḥotp. Temp. Amosis – Amenophis I(?).
13. **SHUROY.** Head of brazier-bearers of Amūn. Ramessid.
14. **ḤUY.** *waʿb*-priest of 'Amenophis, the favourite of Amūn'. Ramessid.
15. **TETIKY.** King's son, Mayor in the Southern City. Early Dyn. XVIII.
16. **PANEḤESI.** Prophet of 'Amenophis of the Forecourt'. Temp. Ramesses II.
17. **NEBAMŪN.** Scribe and physician of the King. Temp. Amenophis II(?).
18. **BAKI.** Chief servant who weighs the silver and gold of the estate of Amūn. Temp. Tuthmosis III or earlier.
19. **AMENMOSI.** First prophet of 'Amenophis of the Forecourt'. Temp. Ramesses I – Sethos I(?).
20. **MENTUḤIRKHOPSHEF.** Fan-bearer, Mayor of Aphroditopolis. Temp. Tuthmosis III(?).
21. **USER.** Steward of Tuthmosis I. Temp. Tuthmosis I.
22. **WAḤ.** Royal butler. Temp. Tuthmosis III(?).
23. **THAY.** Royal scribe of Pharaoh's dispatches. Temp. Merneptaḥ.
24. **NEBAMŪN.** Steward of the royal wife Nebtu. Temp. Tuthmosis III.
25. **AMENEMḤAB.** First prophet of Khons. Ramessid.
26. **KHNEMEMḤAB.** Overseer of the treasury in the Ramesseum in the estate of Amūn. Temp. Ramesses II.

27. **SHESHONK.** Chief steward of the divine adoratress Ankhnesneferebrē῾. Temp. Apries and Amasis.
28. **ḤORI.** Officer of the estate of Amūn. Ramessid.
29. **AMENEMŌPET, called PAIRI.** Governor of the town, vizier. Temp. Amenophis II.
30. **KHENSMOSI.** Scribe of the treasury of the estate of Amūn. Ramessid.
31. **KHONS, called TO.** First prophet of Menkheperrē῾ (Tuthmosis III). Temp. Ramesses II.
32. **D̲ḤUTMOSI.** Chief steward of Amūn, Overseer of the granaries of Upper and Lower Egypt. Temp. Ramesses II.
33. **PEDAMENŌPET.** Prophet, Chief lector. Saite.
34. **MENTUEMḤĒT.** Fourth prophet of Amūn in Thebes. Temp. Taharqa and Psammetikhos.
35. **BEKENKHONS.** First prophet of Amūn. Temp. Ramesses II.
36. **IBI.** Chief steward of the divine adoratress. Temp. Psammetikhos I.
37. **ḤARUA.** Chief steward of the god's wife Amenardais I. Saite.
38. **ZESERKARA῾SONB.** Counter of grain in the granary of divine offerings of Amūn. Temp. Tuthmosis IV.
39. **PUIMRĒ῾.** Second prophet of Amūn. Temp. Tuthmosis III.
40. **AMENḤOTP, called ḤUY.** Viceroy of Kush. Temp. Amenophis IV – Tut῾ankhamūn.
41. **AMENEMŌPET, called IPY.** Chief steward of Amūn in the Southern City. Temp. Ramesses I – Sethos I(?).
42. **AMENMOSI.** Captain of troops. Temp. Tuthmosis III – Amenophis II.
43. **NEFERRONPET.** Overseer of Pharaoh's kitchen. Temp. Amenophis II(?).
44. **AMENEMḤAB.** *wa῾b*-priest-in-front of Amūn. Ramessid.
45. **D̲ḤOUT.** Steward of the First prophet of Amūn, Mery. Amenophis II. Usurped by D̲ḤOUTEMḤAB. Head of the makers of fine linen(?) of the estate of Amūn. Temp. Ramesses II(?).
46. **RA῾MOSI.** Steward, Overseer of the granaries of Upper and Lower Egypt. Temp. Amenophis III(?).
47. **USERḤĒT.** Overseer of the royal harim. Temp. Amenophis III.
48. **AMENEMḤĒT, called SURERO.** Chief steward, Overseer of the cattle of Amūn. Temp. Amenophis III.
49. **NEFERḤŌTEP.** Chief scribe of Amūn. Probably Temp. Ay.
50. **NEFERḤŌTEP.** Divine father of Amen-rē῾. Temp. Ḥaremḥab.
51. **USERḤĒT, called NEFERḤABEF.** First prophet of the royal *ka* of Tuthmosis I. Temp. Sethos I.
52. **NAKHT.** Astronomer of Amūn. Temp. Tuthmosis IV(?).
53. **AMENEMḤĒT.** Agent of Amūn. Temp. Tuthmosis III.
54. **ḤUY.** Sculptor of Amūn. Temp. Tuthmosis IV [Amenophis III(?)]. Usurped by KENRO. *wa῾b*-priest, head of the magazine of Khons. Early Dyn. XIX.
55. **RA῾MOSI.** Governor of the town and vizier. Temp. Amenophis IV.
56. **USERḤĒT.** Royal scribe, Child of the nursery. Temp. Amenophis II.
57. **KHA῾EMḤĒT, called MAḤU.** Overseer of the granaries of Upper and Lower Egypt. Temp. Amenophis III.

58. Name unknown, Temp. Amenophis III. Usurped by AMENḤOTP, Overseer of the prophets of Amūn and son AMENEMŌNET, Temple scribe. Dyn. XX.
59. ḲEN. First prophet of Mut, Mistress of Asher. Early Dyn. XVIII.
60. ANTEFOḲER. Governor of the town and vizier, and wife SENT, Prophetess of Ḥatḥor. Temp. Sesostris I.
61. USER. Governor of the town and vizier. Temp. Tuthmosis III.
62. AMENEMWASKHET. Overseer of the Cabinet. Temp. Tuthmosis III(?).
63. SEBKḤOTP. Mayor of the Southern Lake and the Lake of Sobk. Temp. Tuthmosis IV.
64. ḤEKERNEḤEḤ. Nurse of the King's son Amenḥotp. Temp. Tuthmosis IV.
65. NEBAMŲN. Scribe of the royal accounts, Overseer of the granary. Temp. Ḥatshepsut(?). Usurped by IMISEBA. Head of the altar, Head of the temple-scribes in the estate of Amūn. Temp. Ramesses IX.
66. ḤEPU. Vizier. Temp. Tuthmosis IV.
67. ḤEPUSONB. First prophet of Amūn. Temp. Ḥatshepsut.
68. [PER?]ENKHNUM. *waʿb*-priest of Amūn of Karnak, and of Mut of Asher. Dyn. XX. Usurped by ESPANEFERHOR. Head of temple-scribes of the estate of Amūn.
69. MENNA. Scribe of Pharaoh's fields. Temp. Tuthmosis IV(?).
70. Usurped by AMENMOSI. Overseer of sandal-makers(?) of the estate of Amūn. Dyn. XXI.
71. SENENMUT. Chief steward, Steward of Amūn. Temp. Ḥatshepsut.
72. RĒʿ. First prophet of Amūn in the Mortuary Temple of Tuthmosis III. Temp. Amenophis II.
73. AMENḤOTP(?). Overseer of works on the two great obelisks in the Temple of Amūn, Chief steward. Temp. Ḥatshepsut.
74. THANUNY. Royal scribe, Commander of soldiers. Temp. Tuthmosis IV.
75. AMENḤOTP-SI-SE. Second prophet of Amūn. Temp. Tuthmosis IV.
76. THENUNA. Fan-bearer on the right of the King. Temp. Tuthmosis IV.
77. PTAḤEMḤĒT. Child of the nursery, Overseer of works in the Temple of Amūn, Pharaoh's standard-bearer. Temp. Tuthmosis IV.
78. ḤAREMḤAB. Royal scribe, Scribe of recruits. Temp. Tuthmosis III – Amenophis III.
79. MENKHEPER(RAʿSONB). Overseer of Pharaoh's granary, *waʿb*-priest in the Mortuary temple of Tuthmosis III. Temp. Tuthmosis III – Amenophis II(?)
80. ḎḤUTNŪFER. Overseer of the treasury, Royal scribe. Temp. Amenophis II.
81. INENI. Overseer of the granary of Amūn. Temp. Amenophis I – Tuthmosis III.
82. AMENEMḤĒT. Counter of grain of Amūn, Steward of the vizier. Temp. Tuthmosis III.
83. ʿAMETHU, called ʿAḤMOSI. Governor of the town and vizier. Early temp. Tuthmosis III.

84. **AMUNEZEḤ.** First royal herald, Overseer of the gate. Temp. Tuthmosis III.
85. **AMENEMḤAB, called MAḤU.** Lieutenant-commander of soldiers. Temp. Tuthmosis III – Amenophis II.
86. **MENKHEPERRAʿSONB.** First prophet of Amūn. Temp. Tuthmosis III.
87. **MINNAKHT.** Overseer of the granaries of Upper and Lower Egypt, Overseer of Pharaoh's horses. Temp. Tuthmosis III.
88. **PEḤSUKHER, called THENENU.** Lieutenant of the King, Pharaoh's standard-bearer. Temp. Tuthmosis III – Amenophis II.
89. **AMENMOSI.** Steward in the Southern City. Temp. Amenophis III.
90. **NEBAMŪN.** Standard-bearer of (the sacred bark called) 'Beloved-of-Amūn', Captain of troops of the police on the west of Thebes. Temp. Tuthmosis IV – Amenophis III.
91. **Captain of troops . . ., Overseer of horses.** Temp. Tuthmosis IV – Amenophis III.
92. **SUEMNUT.** Royal butler clean of hands. Temp. Amenophis II.
93. **ḲENAMŪN.** Chief steward of the King. Temp. Amenophis II.
94. **RAʿMOSI, called ʿAMY.** First royal herald, Fan-bearer on the right of the King. Temp. Amenophis II(?).
95. **MERY.** First prophet of Amūn. Temp. Amenophis II.
96. **SENNŪFER.** Mayor of the Southern City. Temp. Amenophis II.
97. **AMENEMḤĒT.** First prophet of Amūn. Temp. Amenophis II(?).
98. **KAEMḤERIBSEN.** Third prophet of Amūn. Temp. Tuthmosis III – Amenophis II(?).
99. **SENNŪFER.** Overseer of the seal, Overseer of the gold-land of Amūn. Temp. Tuthmosis III.
100. **REKHMIRĒʿ.** Governor of the town and Vizier. Temp. Tuthmosis III – Amenophis II.
101. **THANURO.** Royal butler. Temp. Amenophis II.
102. **IMḤOTEP.** Royal scribe, Child of the nursery. Temp. Amenophis III.
103. **DAGI.** Governor of the town and Vizier. End of Dyn. XI.
104. **ḎḤUTNŪFER.** Overseer of the treasury, Royal scribe. Temp. Amenophis II.
105. **KHAʿEMŌPET.** Prophet of the noble ram-sceptre of Amūn. Dyn. XIX.
106. **PASER.** Governor of the town and Vizier. Temp. Sethos ? – Ramesses II.
107. **NEFERSEKHERU.** Royal scribe, Steward of the estate of Amenophis III 'Rēʿ is brilliant'. Temp. Amenophis III.
108. **NEBSENY.** First prophet of Onuris. Temp. Tuthmosis IV(?).
109. **MIN.** Mayor of Thinis, Overseer of the prophets of Onuris. Temp. Tuthmosis III.
110. **ḎḤOUT.** Royal butler, Royal herald. Temp. Ḥatshepsut – Tuthmosis III.
111. **AMENWAḤSU.** Scribe of divine writings in the estate of Amūn. Temp. Ramesses II.
112. **MENKHEPERRAʿSONB.** First prophet of Amūn. Temp. Tuthmosis III. **Usurped by ʿASHEFYTEMWĒSET.** Prophet of Amūn 'Great of Majesty'. Ramessid.

113. **KYNEBU.** *wa'b*-priest over-the-secrets of the estate of Amūn, prophet in the Temple of Tuthmosis IV. Temp. Ramesses VIII.
114. **Head of gold-workers of the estate of Amūn.** Dyn. XX.
115. **Dyn.** XIX.
116. **Hereditary prince.** Temp. Tuthmosis IV – Amenophis III(?).
117. **Dyn.** XI, used by ZEMUTEF 'ANKH, Outline-draughtsman of the House of gold, fashioning the gods of the estate of Amūn. Dyn. XXI–XXII.
118. **AMENMOSI.** Fan-bearer on the right of the King. Temp. Amenophis III(?).
119. **Name lost.** Temp. Ḥatshepsut – Tuthmosis III.
120. **'ANEN.** Second prophet of Amūn. Temp. Amenophis III.
121. **'AḤMOSI.** First lector of Amūn. Temp. Tuthmosis III(?).
122. **AMENḤOTP and AMENEMḤĒT.** Overseers of the magazine of Amūn. Temp. Tuthmosis III.
123. **AMENEMḤĒT.** Overseer of the granary, Counter of bread. Temp. Tuthmosis III.
124. **RĒ'Y.** Overseer of Pharaoh's magazine, Steward of the good god Tuthmosis I. Temp. Tuthmosis I.
125. **DUAUNEḤEḤ.** First herald, Overseer of the estate of Amūn. Temp. Ḥatshepsut.
126. **ḤARMOSI.** Great commander of soldiers of the estate of Amūn. Saite(?).
127. **SENEMI'OḤ.** Royal scribe, Overseer of all that grows. Temp. Tuthmosis III(?), usurped in Ramessid times.
128. **PATHENFY.** Mayor of Edfu, Mayor of the City. Saite.
129. **Name lost.** Temp. Tuthmosis III or IV.
130. **MAY.** Harbour-master in the Southern City. Temp. Tuthmosis III(?).
131. **AMENUSER or USER.** Governor of the town and vizier. Temp. Tuthmosis III.
132. **RA'MOSI.** Great scribe of the King, Overseer of the treasuries of Taharqa. Temp. Taharqa.
133. **NEFERRONPET.** Chief of the weavers in the Ramesseum. Temp. Ramesses II.
134. **THAUENANY, called ANY.** Prophet of Amenophis who navigates on the Sea of Amūn. Dyn. XIX.
135. **BEKENAMŪN.** *wa'b*-priest-in-front of Amūn. Dyn. XIX.
136. **Royal scribe . . . of Pharaoh.** Dyn. XIX.
137. **MOSI.** Head of Pharaoh's works in every monument of Amūn. Ramesses II.
138. **NEZEMGER.** Overseer of the garden in the Ramesseum in the estate of Amūn. Temp. Ramesses II.
139. **PAIRI.** *wa'b*-priest-in-front, Overseer of peasants of Amūn. Temp. Amenophis III.
140. **NEFERRONPET, probably called KEFIA.** Goldworker, Portrait sculptor. Temp. Tuthmosis III – Amenophis II.
141. **BEKENKHONS.** *wa'b*-priest of Amūn. Ramessid.
142. **SIMUT.** Overseer of works of Amen-Rē' in Karnak. Temp. Tuthmosis III – Amenophis II(?).

143. **Name lost.** Temp. Tuthmosis III – Amenophis II(?).
144. **NU.** Head of field-labourers. Temp. Tuthmosis III(?).
145. **NEBAMŪN.** Head of bowmen. Dyn. XVIII.
146. **NEBAMŪN.** Overseer of the granary of Amūn. Tuthmosis III(?).
147. **Head of the master of ceremonies(?) of Amūn.** Temp. Tuthmosis IV(?).
148. **AMENEMŌPET.** Prophet of Amūn. Temp. Ramesses III–V.
149. **AMENMOSI.** Royal scribe of Pharaoh's table, Overseer of the huntsmen of Amūn. Ramessid.
150. **USERḤĒT.** Overseer of cattle of Amūn. Late Dyn. XVIII.
151. **ḤETY.** Counter of cattle of the god's wife of Amūn, Steward of the god's wife. Temp. Tuthmosis IV.
152. **Name lost.** Late Dyn. XVIII. Usurped in Ramessid times (?).
153. **Name lost.** Temp. Sethos I(?).
154. **TATI.** Butler. Temp. Tuthmosis III(?).
155. **ANTEF.** Great herald of the King. Temp. Ḥatshepsut – Tuthmosis III.
156. **PENNESUTTAUI.** Captain of troops, Governor of the South Lands. Dyn. XIX.
157. **NEBWENENEF.** First prophet of Amūn. Temp. Ramesses II.
158. **THONŪFER.** Third prophet of Amūn. Probably Temp. Ramesses III.
159. **RAʿYA.** Fourth prophet of Amūn. Dyn. XIX.
160. **BESENMUT.** True royal acquaintance. Saite.
161. **NAKHT.** Bearer of floral offerings to Amūn. Temp. Amenophis III(?).
162. **ḲENAMŪN.** Mayor in the Southern City, Overseer of the granary of Amūn. Dyn. XVIII.
163. **AMENEMḤĒT.** Mayor of the Southern City, Royal scribe. Dyn. XIX.
164. **ANTEF.** Scribe of recruits. Temp. Tuthmosis III.
165. **NEḤEMʿAWAY.** Goldworker and portrait sculptor. Temp. Tuthmosis IV(?).
166. **RAʿMOSI.** Overseer of works in Karnak, Overseer of cattle. Dyn. XX.
167. **Name lost.** Dyn. XVIII.
168. **ANY.** Divine father clean of hands, Chosen lector of the lord of the gods. Dyn. XIX.
169. **SENNA.** Head of the goldworkers of Amūn. Temp. Amenophis II.
170. **NEBMEḤYT.** Scribe of recruits of the Ramesseum in the estate of Amūn. Temp. Ramesses II.
171. **Name lost.** Dyn. XVIII.
172. **MENTIYWY.** Royal butler, Child of the nursery. Temp. Tuthmosis IV – Amenophis II(?).
173. **KHAʿY.** Scribe of the divine offerings of the Gods of Thebes. Dyn. XIX.
174. **ʿASHAKHET.** Priest-in-front of Mut. Dyn. XIX.
175. **No name.** Temp. Tuthmosis IV(?).
176. **USERḤĒT.** Servant of Amūn. Temp. Amenophis II – Tuthmosis IV.
177. **AMENEMŌPET.** Scribe of truth in the Ramesseum in the estate of Amūn. Temp. Ramesses II(?).
178. **NEFERRONPET, called KENRO.** Scribe of the treasury in the estate of Amen-rēʿ. Temp. Ramesses II.

179. **NEBAMŪN.** Counter of grain in the granary of divine offerings of Amūn. Temp. Ḥatshepsut.
180. **No name.** Dyn. XIX.
181. **NEBAMŪN,** Pharaoh's head sculptor, and **IPUKY,** Pharaoh's sculptor. Temp. Amenophis III–IV.
182. **AMENEMḤĒT.** Scribe of the mat. Temp. Tuthmosis III.
183. **NEBSUMENU.** Chief steward, Steward in the house of Ramesses II. Temp. Ramesses II.
184. **NEFERMENU.** Mayor in the Southern City, Royal scribe. Temp. Ramesses II.
185. **SENIOḲER.** Hereditary prince, Divine chancellor. First Intermediate Period.
186. **IḤY.** Nomarch. First Intermediate Period.
187. **PAKHIḤĒT.** *waʿb*-priest of Amūn. Dyn. XIX.
188. **PARENNŪFER.** Royal butler clean of hands, Steward. Temp. Amenophis IV.
189. **NEKHT-D̠ḤOUT.** Overseer of carpenters on the northern lake of Amūn, Head of goldworkers in the estate of Amūn. Temp. Ramesses II.
190. **ESBANEBDED.** Divine father, Prophet at the head of the King. Saite.
191. **WEḤEBRĒʿ-NEBPEḤTI.** Chamberlain of the divine adoratress, Director of the festival. Temp. Psammetikhos I.
192. **KHARUEF, called SENAʿA.** Steward of the great royal wife Teye. Temp. Amenophis III–IV.
193. **PTAḤEMḤEB.** Magnate of the seal in the treasury of the estate of Amūn. Dyn. XIX.
194. **D̠ḤUTEMḤAB.** Overseer of the marshland-dwellers of the estate of Amūn. Dyn. XIX.
195. **BEKENAMŪN.** Scribe of the treasury of the estate of Amūn. Dyn. XIX.
196. **PEDEḤORRESNET.** Chief steward of Amūn. Saite.
197. **PEDENEITH.** Chief steward of the god's wife, the divine adoratress Ankhnesneferebrēʿ. Temp. Psammetikhos II.
198. **RIYA.** Head of the magazine of Amūn in Karnak. Ramessid.
199. **AMENARNOFRU.** Overseer of the magazine. Dyn. XVIII.
200. **DEDI.** Governor of the deserts on the west of Thebes, Head of the regiment of Pharaoh. Temp. Tuthmosis III – Amenophis II.
201. **REʿ.** First royal herald. Temp. Tuthmosis IV – Amenophis III.
202. **NEKHTAMŪN.** Prophet of Ptaḥ Lord of Thebes, Priest-in-front of Amūn. Dyn. XIX(?).
203. **UNNŪFER.** Divine father of Mut. Dyn. XIX.
204. **NEBʿANENSU.** Sailor of the first prophet of Amūn. Dyn. XVIII.
205. **D̠ḤUTMOSI.** Royal butler. Temp. Tuthmosis III(?) – Amenophis II(?).
206. **INPUEMḤAB.** Scribe of the Place of Truth. Ramessid.
207. **ḤAREMḤAB.** Scribe of divine offerings of Amūn. Ramessid.
208. **ROMA.** Divine father of Amen-rēʿ. Ramessid.
209. **SEREMḤATREKHYT.** Hereditary prince, Sole beloved friend. Saite.
210. **RAʿWEBEN.** Servant in the Place of Truth. Dyn. XIX.
211. **PANEB.** Servant of Pharaoh in the Place of Truth. Dyn. XIX.

212. **RAʿMOSI.** Scribe in the Place of Truth. Temp. Ramesses II.
213. **PENAMŪN.** Servant of Pharaoh, Servant in the Place of Truth. Dyn. XX.
214. **KHAWI.** Custodian in the Place of Truth, Servant of Amūn in Luxor. Ramessid.
215. **AMENEMŌPET.** Royal scribe in the Place of Truth. Dyn. XIX.
216. **NEFERḤŌTEP.** Foreman. Temp. Ramesses II – Sethos II.
217. **IPUY.** Sculptor. Temp. Ramesses II.
218. **AMENNAKHT.** Servant in the Place of Truth on the west of Thebes. Ramessid.
219. **NEBENMAʿET.** Servant in the Place of Truth on the west of Thebes. Ramessid.
220. **KHAʿEMTERI.** Servant in the Place of Truth. Ramessid.
221. **ḤORIMIN.** Scribe of soldiers in the palace of the King on the west of Thebes. Ramessid.
222. **ḤEKAMAʿETRĒʿ-NAKHT, called TURO.** First prophet of Monthu, Lord of Thebes. Temp. Ramesses III–IV.
223. **KARAKHAMŪN.** First *ʿaḳ*-priest. Saite.
224. **ʿAḤMOSI, called ḤUMAY.** Overseer of the estate of the god's wife, Overseer of the two granaries of the god's wife Aḥmosi Nefertere. Temp. Tuthmosis III or Ḥatshepsut.
225. **A First prophet of Ḥatḥor.** Temp. Tuthmosis III(?).
226. **ḤEKARESHU.** Royal scribe, Overseer of the royal nurses. Temp. Amenophis III.
227. **Name lost.** Temp. Tuthmosis III.
228. **AMENMOSI.** Scribe of the treasury of Amūn. Dyn. XVIII.
229. **Name lost.** Dyn. XVIII.
230. **Perhaps MEN.** Scribe of Pharaoh's soldiers. Dyn. XVIII.
231. **NEBAMŪN.** Counter of the grain of Amūn in the granary of divine offerings. Early Dyn. XVIII.
232. **THARWAS.** Scribe of the divine seal of the treasury of Amūn.
233. **SAROY.** Royal scribe of Pharaoh's table. Ramessid.
234. **ROY.** Mayor. Dyn. XVIII or XIX.
235. **USERḤĒT.** First prophet of Monthu Lord of Thebes. Dyn XX.
236. **ḤARNAKHT.** Second prophet of Amūn, Overseer of the treasury of Amūn. Ramessid.
237. **UNNŪFER.** Chief lector. Ramessid.
238. **NEFERWEBEN.** Royal butler clean of hands. Dyn. XVIII.
239. **PENḤET.** Governor of all Northern Lands. Temp. Tuthmosis IV – Amenophis III(?).
240. **MERU.** Overseer of sealers. Temp. Mentuḥotp-Nebḥepetrē.
241. **ʿAḤMOSI.** Scribe of divine writings, Child of the nursery, Head of mysteries in the House of the morning. Temp. Tuthmosis III(?).
242. **WEḤEBRĒʿ.** Chamberlain of the divine adoratress Ankhnesneferebrēʿ. Saite.
243. **PEMU.** Mayor of the Southern City. Saite.
244. **PAKHARU.** Overseer of carpenters of the Temple of Amūn. Ramessid.
245. **ḤORY.** Steward of the royal wife. Dyn. XVIII.

246. **SENENRĒʿ.** Scribe, Chief of weavers(?) of Amūn. Dyn. XVIII.
247. **SIMUT.** Counter of the cattle of Amūn. Dyn. XVIII.
248. **D̠ḤUTMOSI.** Maker of offerings of Tuthmosis III. Dyn. XVIII.
249. **NEFERRONPET.** Supplier of sweets in the Temple of Nebmaʿetrēʿ. Temp. Tuthmosis IV – Amenophis III.
250. **RAʿMOSI.** Scribe in the Place of Truth. Temp. Ramesses II.
251. **AMENMOSI.** Royal scribe, Overseer of the cattle of Amūn, Overseer of the magazine of Amūn. Temp. early Tuthmosis III.
252. **SENIMEN.** Steward, Nurse of the god's wife. Temp. Ḥatshepsut.
253. **KHNEMMOSI.** Counter of grain in the granary of Amūn and in the granary of divine offerings. Temp. Amenophis III(?).
254. **MOSI.** Scribe of the treasury, Custodian of the estate of Teye in the estate of Amūn. Late Dyn. XVIII.
255. **ROY.** Royal scribe, Steward in the estates of Ḥaremḥab and of Amūn. Temp. Ḥaremḥab(?).
256. **NEBENKEMET.** Overseer of the cabinet, Fanbearer, Child of the nursery. Temp. Amenophis II.
257. **NEFERḤŌTEP.** Counter of grain of Amūn. Temp. Tuthmosis IV – Amenophis III. Usurped by MAḤU, Deputy in the Ramesseum. Temp. Ramesses II.
258. **MENKHEPER.** Child of the nursery, Royal scribe of the house of the royal children. Temp. Tuthmosis IV(?).
259. **ḤORI.** Scribe in all the monuments in the estate of Amūn, Head of the outline-draughtsmen in the House of Gold of the estate of Amūn. Ramessid.
260. **USER.** Weigher of Amūn, Overseer of the ploughed lands of Amūn. Temp. Tuthmosis III(?).
261. **KHAʿEMWĒSET.** *waʿb*-priest of Amenophis I. Dyn. XVIII.
262. **An overseer of fields.** Temp. Tuthmosis III(?).
263. **PIAY.** Scribe of the granary in the Temple of Amūn, Scribe of accounts in the Ramesseum. Temp. Ramesses II.
264. **IPIY.** Overseer of cattle, Chief of the Pharaoh. Dyn. XIX.
265. **AMENEMŌPET.** Royal scribe in the Place of Truth. Dyn. XIX.
266. **AMENNAKHT.** Pharaoh's chief craftsman in the Place of Truth on the west of Thebes. Dyn. XIX.
267. **ḤAY.** Officer of the workmen in the Place of Truth on the west of Thebes, Fashioner of the images of all the gods in the House of Gold. Dyn. XX.
268. **NEBNAKHT.** Servant in the Place of Truth. Dyn. XIX.
269. **Name lost.** Ramessid.
270. **AMENEMWIA.** *waʿb*-priest, lector of Ptaḥ-Sokari. Dyn. XIX.
271. **NAY.** Royal scribe. Temp. Ay.
272. **KHAʿEMŌPET.** Divine father of Amūn in the west, Lector in the Temple of Sokari. Ramessid.
273. **SAYEMIOTF.** Scribe in the estate of his lord. Ramessid.
274. **AMENWAḤSU.** First prophet of Monthu of Tod, and of Thebes, *sem*-priest in the Ramesseum in the estate of Amūn. Ramessid.
275. **SEBKMOSI.** Head *waʿb*-priest, Divine father in the Temples of Amenophis III, and of Sokari. Ramessid.

276. **AMENEMŌPET.** Overseer of the treasury of gold and silver, Judge, Overseer of the cabinet. Temp. Tuthmosis IV(?).
277. **AMENEMŌNET.** Divine father of the mansion of Amenophis III. Ramessid.
278. **AMENEMḤAB.** Herdsman of Amen-Rēʿ. Ramessid.
279. **PABASA.** Chief steward of the god's wife. Temp. Psammetikhos I.
280. **MEKETRĒʿ.** Chief steward in . . ., Chancellor. Temp. Mentuḥotp (Sʿankhkarēʿ).
281. **Unfinished temple of Mentuḥotp-Sʿankhkarēʿ.**
282. **NAKHTMIN.** Head of bowmen, Overseer of the South Lands. Ramessid.
283. **ROMA.** First prophet of Amūn. Temp. Ramesses II – Sethos II.
284. **PAḤEMNETER.** Scribe of the offerings of the gods. Ramessid.
285. **INY.** Head of the magazine of Mut. Ramessid.
286. **NIAY.** Scribe of the table. Ramessid.
287. **PENDUA.** *waʿb*-priest of Amūn. Ramessid.
288. **BEKENKHONS.** Scribe of the divine book of Khons. Ramessid.
289. **SETAU.** Viceroy of Kush, Overseer of the South Lands. Temp. Ramesses II.
290. **IRINŪFER.** Servant in the Place of Truth on the West. Ramessid.
291. **NU.** Servant in the Great Place, and **NEKHTMIN.** Servant in the Place of Truth. Late Dyn. XVIII.
292. **PESHEDU.** Servant in the Place of Truth. Temp. Sethos I – Ramesses II.
293. **RAʿMESSENAKHT.** First prophet of Amūn. Temp. Ramesses IV.
294. **AMENḤOTP.** Overseer of the granary of Amūn. Temp. Amenophis III. Usurped by ROMA. *waʿb*-priest of Amūn. Early Ramessid.
295. **Ḏ̣HUTMOSI, called PAROY.** Head of the secrets in the chest of Anubis, *sem*-priest in the Good House, Embalmer. Temp. Tuthmosis IV – Amenophis III(?).
296. **NEFERSEKHERU.** Scribe of the divine offerings of all the gods, Officer of the treasury . . . in the Southern City. Ramessid.
297. **AMENEMŌPET, called THONŪFER.** Counter of grain of Amūn, Overseer of fields. Early Dyn. XVIII.
298. **BAKI.** Foreman in the Place of Truth, and father (?) of **UNNŪFER. Pharaoh's servant in the Place of Truth. Ramessid.**
299. **INHERKHAʿ.** Pharaoh's foreman in the Place of Truth. Temp. Ramesses III–IV.
300. **ʿANḤOTP.** Viceroy of Kush, Governor of the South Lands, Scribe of Pharaoh's table. Ramessid.
301. **ḤORI.** Scribe of Pharaoh's table in the estate of Amūn. Ramessid.
302. **PARAʿEMḤAB.** Overseer of the magazine. Ramessid.
303. **PASER.** Head of the magazine of Amūn, Third prophet of Amūn. Dyn. XIX–XX.
304. **PIAY.** Scribe of the table of Amūn, Pharaoh's scribe. Ramessid.
305. **PASER.** *waʿb*-priest-in-front of Amūn, Scribe of the divine offerings of Amūn. Dyn. XIX–XXI.
306. **IRZANEN.** Door-opener of the estate of Amūn. Dyn. XIX–XXI.

307. **THONŪFER**. Dyn. XX–XXI.
308. **KEMSIT**. Unique royal concubine, Prophetess of Ḥatḥor. Temp. Mentuḥotp (Nebḥepetrēʿ).
309. **Name unknown.** Dyn. XIX-XXI.
310. **A Chancellor of the King of Lower Egypt.** Dyn. XI.
311. **KHETY**. Seal-bearer of the King of Lower Egypt. Temp. Mentuḥotp-Nebḥepetrēʿ.
312. **ESPEKASHUTI.** Governor of the town and vizier. Saite.
313. **ḤENENU**. Great steward. Temp. Mentuḥotp-Nebḥepetrēʿ and Mentuḥotp-Sʿankhkarēʿ.
314. **ḤARḤOTP.** Seal-bearer of the King of Lower Egypt, Henchman. Dyn. XI.
315. **IPI.** Governor of the town and vizier, Judge. Temp. Mentuḥotp-Nebḥepetrēʿ.
316. **NEFERḤŌTEP.** Custodian of the bow. Dyn. XI.
317. **ḎḤUTNŪFER.** Scribe of the counting of corn in the granary of divine offerings of Amūn. Temp. Tuthmosis III(?).
318. **AMENMOSI.** Necropolis-stonemason of Amūn. Temp. Tuthmosis III(?).
319. **NOFRU**. Daughter of Mentuḥotp-Sʿankhibtaui, and **IʿOḤ**. Wife of Mentuḥotp-Nebḥepetrēʿ.
320. **INḤAʿPI.** Perhaps wife of Amosis.
321. **KHAʿEMŌPET**. Servant in the Place of Truth. Ramessid.
322. **PENSHENʿABU**. Servant in the Place of Truth. Ramessid.
323. **PESHEDU**. Outline-draughtsman of Amūn in the Place of Truth, and in the Temple of Sokari. Temp. Sethos I.
324. **ḤATIAY**. Overseer of the prophets of all the gods, Chief prophet of Sobk, Scribe of the Temple of Monthu. Ramessid.
325. **Possibly SMEN**. Dyn. XVIII.
326. **PESHEDU**. Foreman. Ramessid.
327. **TUROBAY**. Servant in the Place of Truth. Ramessid.
328. **ḤAY**. Servant in the Place of Truth. Temp. Ramesses III.
329. **MOSI, MOSI and IPY**. Servants in the Place of Truth. Ramessid.
330. **KARO**. Servant in the Place of Truth. Dyn. XIX.
331. **PENNE, called SUNERO**. Chief prophet of Monthu. Ramessid.
332. **PENERNUTET**. Chief watchman of the granary of the estate of Amūn. Ramessid.
333. **Name lost**. Temp. Amenophis III(?).
334. **A Chief of husbandmen**. Temp. Amenophis III(?).
335. **NEKHTAMŪN**. *waʿb*-priest of Amenophis (I), Chiseller of Amūn, Servant in the Place of Truth. Dyn. XIX.
336. **NEFERRONPET**. Servant in the Place of Truth. Dyn. XIX.
337. **ḲEN**. Chiseller in the Place of Truth. Temp. Ramesses II. Usurped by ESKHONS. Dyn. XXI or XXII.
338. **MAY**. Outline-draughtsman of Amūn. Late Dyn. XVIII.
339. **ḤUY**. Servant in the Place of Truth, and **PESHEDU**, Servant in the Place of Truth, Necropolis-stonemason of Amūn in Karnak. Temp. Ramesses II.

340. **AMENEMḤĒT.** Servant in the Place of Truth. Early Dyn. XVIII.
341. **NEKHTAMŪN.** Head of the altar in the Ramesseum. Temp. Ramesses II.
342. **ḎḤUTMOSI.** Hereditary prince, Royal herald. Temp. Tuthmosis III.
343. **BENIA, called PAḤEKMEN.** Overseer of works, Child of the nursery. Early Dyn. XVIII.
344. **PIAY.** Overseer of the herds of Amen-rēʿ in the Southern City, Royal scribe of the herds of Amenophis I. Ramessid.
345. **AMENḤOTP.** *waʿb*-priest, Eldest king's son of Tuthmosis I. Temp. Tuthmosis I.
346. **AMENḤOTP.** Overseer of the women of the royal harim of the divine adoratress Tentopet. Temp. Ramesses IV.
347. **ḤORI.** Scribe of the nome. Ramessid.
348. **A Chief steward, Mayor.** Dyn. XVIII. Usurped by NAʿAMUTNAKHT. Door-opener of the House of Gold of Amūn. Dyn. XXII.
349. **THAY.** Overseer of fowl-houses. Early Dyn. XVIII.
350. **. . . Y. Scribe of the counting of bread.** Dyn. XVIII.
351. **ABAU.** Scribe of horses. Ramessid.
352. **An Overseer of the granary of Amūn.** Ramessid.
353. **SENENMUT.** Chief steward, Steward of Amūn. Temp. Ḥatshepsut.
354. **Perhaps AMENEMḤĒT.** Early Dyn. XVIII.
355. **Perhaps AMENPAḤAʿPI.** Servant in the Place of Truth. Dyn. XX.
356. **AMENEMWIA.** Servant in the Place of Truth. Dyn. XIX.
357. **ḎḤUTIḤIRMAKTUF.** Servant in the Place of Truth. Dyn. XIX.
358. **ʿAHMOSI MERYTAMŪN.** Daughter of Tuthmosis III, Wife of Amenophis II.
359. **INHERKHAʿ.** Pharaoh's foreman in the Place of Truth. Temp. Ramesses III–IV.
360. **ḲAḤA.** Foreman in the Place of Truth. Temp. Ramesses II.
361. **ḤUY.** Great carpenter in the Place of Truth. Temp. Sethos I.
362. **PAʿANEMWESET.** *waʿb*-priest of Amūn. Late Dyn. XIX.
363. **PARAʿEMḤAB.** Overseer of the singers of Amūn. Late Dyn. XIX.
364. **AMENEMḤAB.** Scribe of the divine offerings of all the divinities of Thebes, Scribe of the granary of Amūn. Dyn. XIX.
365. **NEFERMENU.** Overseer of the wig-makers of Amūn in Karnak, Scribe of the treasury of Amūn. Temp. Tuthmosis III.
366. **ZAR.** Custodian of the King's harim. Temp. Mentuḥotp-Nebḥepetrēʿ.
367. **PASER.** Head of bowmen, Child of the Nursery. Companion of his Majesty. Temp. Amenophis II.
368. **AMENḤOTP, called ḤUY.** Overseer of sculptors of Amūn in the Southern City. Late Dyn. XVIII.
369. **KAEMWĒSET.** First prophet of Ptaḥ, Third prophet of Amūn. Dyn. XIX.
370. **A Royal scribe.** Ramessid.
371. **Name unknown.** Ramessid.
372. **AMENKHAʿU.** Overseer of carpenters of the Temple of Medînet Habu. Temp. Ramesses III.

373. **AMENMESSU.** Scribe of Pharaoh's altar. Ramessid.
374. **AMENEMŌPET.** Scribe of the treasury in the Ramesseum. Dyn. XIX.
375. **Name unknown.** Ramessid.
376. **Name lost.** Dyn. XVIII.
377. **Name lost.** Ramessid.
378. **Name unknown.** Dyn. XIX.
379. **Name lost.** Ramessid.
380. **ʿANKHEFEN-RĒʿ-ḤARAKHTI.** Chief in Thebes. Ptolemaic.
381. **Perhaps AMENEMŌNET.** Messenger of the King to every land. Ramessid.
382. **USERMONTU.** Overseer of cattle, Overseer of the treasury. Ramessid.
383. **MERYMOSI.** Viceroy of Kush, son of Amenophis III.
384. **NEBMEḤYT.** Priest of Amūn in the Ramesseum. Dyn. XIX.
385. **ḤUNŪFER.** Mayor of the Southern City, Overseer of the granary of divine offerings of Amūn. Ramessid.
386. **ANTEF.** Chancellor of the King of Lower Egypt, Overseer of soldiers. Middle Kingdom.
387. **MERYPTAḤ.** Royal scribe of Pharaoh's table in Karnak. Temp. Ramesses II.
388. **No texts.** Saite.
389. **BASA.** Chamberlain of Min, Mayor of the Southern City. Saite.
390. **IRTERAU.** Female scribe, Chief attendant of the divine adoratress Nitocris. Temp. Psammetikhos I.
391. **KARABASAKEN.** Prophet of Khonsemwēset-Neferḥōtep, Fourth prophet of Amūn, Mayor of the City. Probably Dyn. XXV.
392. **Name unknown.** Saite(?).
393. **Name unknown.** Early Dyn. XVIII.
394. **No texts.** Ramessid.
395. **Name lost.** Ramessid.
396. **Name unknown.** Dyn. XVIII.
397. **NAKHT.** *waʿb*-priest of Amūn, Overseer of the magazine of Amūn, First King's son of Amūn. Dyn. XVIII(?).
398. **KAMOSI, called NENTOWAREF.** Child of the nursery. Dyn. XVIII.
399. **No name.** Ramessid.
400. **No texts.**
401. **NEBSENY.** Overseer of goldsmiths of Amūn. Temp. Tuthmosis III–IV.
402. **Name unknown.** Temp. Tuthmosis IV – Amenophis III.
403. **MERYMAʿET.** Temple-scribe, Steward. Dyn. XVIII(?).
404. **AKHAMENERAU.** Chief steward of the divine adoratrice. Temp. Amenardais I and Shepenwept II. Dyn. XXV.
405. **KHENTI.** Nomarch. First Intermediate Period.
406. **PIAY.** Scribe of Pharaoh's offering table in the Temple of Amūn. Ramesses II(?).
407. **BINTENDUANŪTER.** Chamberlain of the divine adoratress. Saite.
408. **BEKENAMŪN.** Head of servants of the estate of Amūn. Ramessid.
409. **SIMUT, called KYKY.** Counter of cattle of the estate of Amūn. Temp. Ramesses II.

410. **MUTIRDAIS.** Chief follower of the divine adoratress. Temp. Psammetikhos I.
411. **PSAMMETIKHOS.**
412. **KENAMŪN.** Royal scribe. Tuthmosis III – Amenophis II.
413. **UNASʿANKH.** Royal chamberlain, Overseer of Upper Egypt, Overseer of the two granaries. First Intermediate Period (or earlier).
414. **ʿANKHḤOR.** Governor of Oxyrhyncus, Bahriya Oasis and Memphis, Chief steward of the divine adoratress. Temp. Nitokris.
415. **AMENḤOTP.** Chief physician. Dyn. XIX.

TOMBS THE EXACT LOCATION OF WHICH IS NO LONGER KNOWN:

A1. **AMENEMḤĒT.** *ka*-servant. Dyn. XVIII.
A2. **Anonymous.** Dyn. XVII(?).
A3. **RURU.** Chief of police. New Kingdom.
A4. **WENSU.** Counter of grain. Temp. Tuthmosis III.
A5. **NEFERḤŌTEP.** Overseer of the granary. Probably Temp. Tuthmosis III – Amenophis II.
A6. **ḎḤOUTNŪFER, called SESHU.** Overseer of Pharaoh's marsh-lands. Temp. Tuthmosis III.
A7. **AMENḤOTP.** Counter . . . Dyn. XVIII.
A8. **AMENEMḤAB.** Royal scribe, Steward in the mansion of Amenophis I, Mayor of Thebes, Overseer of the granary of Amūn in Karnak. Late Dyn. XVIII.
A9. **Anonymous.** Temp. Amenophis II.
A10. **ḎḤOUTNŪFER.** Royal scribe, Overseer of the treasury, Chief lector in the embalming house. Early Dyn. XVIII.
A11. **KHAʿEMWĒSET. . . . of Amūn.** New Kingdom.
A12. **NEBWENENEF.** Overseer of marsh-land dwellers of the estate of Amūn. Ramessid(?).
A13. **PAIMOSI.** Sealer of the storehouse of gifts. Dyn. XVIII.
A14. **Anonymous.** Temp. Ramesses II(?).
A15. **AMENEMIB.** Head of the door-keepers in the estate of Amūn. Ramessid.
A16. **ḎḤOUTIḤOTP.** Royal scribe, Steward of the Southern City. Ramessid.
A17. **USERḤĒT.** Head of the measurers of the granary of the estate of Amūn. Temp. Ramesses III.
A18. **AMENEMŌPET.** Prophet of Amen-rēʿ, Secretary, Chief of the scribes in the estate of Amūn. Ramessid.
A19. **AMENḤOTP(?).** Hereditary prince of Thinis, Overseer of the prophets of Onuris. Dyn. XVIII.
A20. **NAKHT.** Overseer of the granary of Amūn. Temp. Amosis.
A21. **Anonymous.** Temp. Amenophis III(?).
A22. **NEFERḤABEF.** Counter of grain. Dyn. XVIII.

A23. PENʿASHEFI. Divine father of Amen-rēʿ, Great of Respect, and of Mut, Great (writer?) of letters, Overseer of the treasury. Ramessid.
A24. SIMUT. Second prophet of Amūn, Overseer of the treasury of gold and silver, Sealer of every contract in Karnak. Temp. Amenophis III.
A25. Anonymous. Dyn. XVIII.
A26. Anonymous. Ramessid.
A27. SAY. Royal scribe of Pharaoh's altar. New Kingdom.
A28. NAKHT(?). Dyn. XIX.
B1. MAḤUḤY. *waʿb*-priest of Amūn in Karnak. Temp. Ramesses III.
B2. AMENNOFRU. *waʿb*-priest-in-front. Temp. Tuthmosis III.
B3. HAUF. Head of the kitchen in the estate of Amūn. Saite(?).
B4 = TT 41.
B5 = TT386.
C1. AMENḤOTP. Overseer of carpenters of Amūn, Chamberlain. Temp. Amenophis III.
C2. AMENEMḤĒT. Noble at the head of the people. Temp. Amosis and Amenophis I.
C3. AMENḤOTP. Deputy of the overseer of the seal. Dyn. XVIII(?).
C4. MERYMAʿET. *waʿb*-priest of Maʿet. Temp. Amenophis III(?) [re-discovered].
C5. Anonymous. Late Dyn. XVIII(?).
C6. IPY. Overseer of boats in the temple of Tuthmosis IV. Temp. Tuthmosis IV.
C7. ḤARMOSI. Head custodian of the treasury in the King's mansion on the west of Thebes. Temp. Ramesses II.
C8. NAKHT. Overseer of fowl-houses in the estate of Amūn. Dyn. XVIII.
C9. [non existent].
C10. PENRENNU. Scribe of the offering table. Dyn. XVIII.
C11. NEBSENY. Overseer of the gold-workers of Amūn, Overseer of all works of silver and gold. Temp. Tuthmosis III(?).
C12. MAḤU. Overseer of the gate.
C13. Anonymous.
C14. ʿANKHEFENḎḤOUT, called NEFEREBRĒʿ-SONB. Saite.
C15. An Overseer of the Two Houses of gold, Overseer of the Two Houses of Silver. Dyn. XVIII.
D1. NEḤI. Viceroy, Governor of the South Lands. Temp. Tuthmosis III.
D2. PETERSUEMḤEBSED. New Kingdom.
D3. MAḤU. Steward of . . . Dyn. XVIII(?).

INDEX

Note Numbers in **bold** type refer to figure numbers.

A General

Abydos 18, 21, 27, 28, 40–1, 52, 71, 80, 84, 87, 89, **11**, **33**
agriculture 35, 38–9, 50, 60, 65, 75, 80, 87
'alabaster' 2
Amarna Period 47, 57, 61, 63, 64, 110
Amūn 21, 45, 61, 84, 92
Amūn-Rēʿ 35
angling 64
anonymous tomb (TT 175) 57–8, **48**
Antiquities Service 115, 126
Anubis 58, 80
Anukis 80
Apis bull 115
archaising look 85–6
archery 63, **27**
architectural drawings 14
arts and crafts 57, 65
Asâsîf 2, 56ff, 67, 74, 84ff, **18**

ba 7ff, 11, **10**
baboons 52
baking 18, 21, 52
banquet scenes 14, 18, 28, 31, 36, 41ff, 52–3, 57, 58, 59, 109
barbers 50
bear 52
bed 44, 81, 89, **36**
bedroom 18
beekeeping 88, 89
beer 10, 45
beeswax 14
Benu-bird 83
Berlin fragments 60–1, 117, 120
Bes 83
boat-builders 88
boats 22
Book of the Dead 65, 78, 83
Book of Gates 65, 72, 81, 85, **51**
Books of Night and Day 89
Books of the Underworld 65, 66, 76, 85
bouquet of Amūn 46, **37**
bread 10, 46
brewing 18
brickmakers 52
British Museum fragments 59ff, 104, 110–1, 113, 117, **35**, **49**
butchers 35
butlers 35, 39

cache 89–90, **75**
cakes 10
camera lucida 106, 107, 109, 111
carpenters 33, 80, **19**
cat 83, **51**
cattle 21, 35
chariotmakers 33, 84, **27**
Chicago House 125–6
children 83
Christianity 4, 92
colours 13, 57, 66, 68, 79, 81
cooking 72
Coptic monuments 21, 92
cornflowers 81
Cretans 33
crocodile 35
cubit rod 81

dancers 18, 88, 119
date juice 45
dates 81
Deir el-Baḥri 19, 24, 27, 56, 84, 89, 90, 92, 121, 123, **75**
Deir el-Bakhît 92
Deir el-Medîna 2, 12, 16, 46ff, 67, 79ff, 90, 94, 114, 119, 125, 130
divine adoratress 88
Djeme 92
dog 92
dôm-palm 12, 81, 92
donkey 75
donkey dung 12
Draʿ Abû el-Nagaʿ 2, 14, 28, 46, 58ff, 67, 74ff, 92, 109, 112, 116–7, 121, 124, **61**
draughts 70, 72
drum 35
duck 36, 76

eggs 81, 122
eggwhite 14
el-Amarna 52, 56, 57, 69
elephant 52
el-Kâb 14
el-Qurn 2
el-Tarif 17
embalming house 9, 40
embalming materials 21
Eros 42
eroticism 36–7
eternity 7, 80

false door 6, **9**
Fayûm 24
Feast of the Valley 35, 45ff, 84, 88, 110, 126
festivals 63
fields of Iaru (rushes) 9, 10, 80, 81
firman 99
First Intermediate Period 19
fish 59, 64, 89
fishing 21, 80
fishing and fowling 14, 18, 27, 35–6, 37, 60, 64, 109, **28**
fishing net 104
fish mummy 81
fowl 10, 46, 80, 89
fowling 30, 36
fox 50
funeral procession 39ff, 41, 51, 57, 66, 72, 76, 87, 88, 89, 110, **11**
funerary beliefs 6ff, 31
funerary canopy 91, **77**
funerary cones 15–6, 30, 48, 76, 84, **14**
funerary equipment 80, 81, **11**
funerary rites 52
furniture 28, 47, 51

garden 61, 62, 80, 99
gardener 65
gardening 21
giraffe 52
Gîza 17
gloves 63

glue 80
god's wives 88
'gold of honour' 76
goldsmith 88
goose 36, 59
granary 14, 18, 21, 27, 39, 60
granary officials, duties of 35
grape ceiling 54, **46**
grid 14, **13**
gum 14
gypsum 12, 66

hair 41, 43, 82, 83, **69**
harpists 18, 64, 70, 72, **22**
harpist's songs 62, 70
harvest festival 35
harvesting 21, 39, 50, **93**
Ḥatḥor 18, 67, 80, 83, 84, 85, 89, **88**
Ḥatḥor cow 65, 66, 67, 72, 76, **53**
hawk 92, 117
herbs 10, 47, 58
Hereafter 6, 9, 10, 18, 39, 49, 57, 65, 70, 72, 83, **8**
high priests of Amūn, duties of 33
hippopotamus 31, 37, 59
hoe 104
horses 60, 78, **66**
Ḥorus 9, 76, 85
houses (ancient) 4, 6, 29
hunting 27, 31, 37ff, 49, 50, 56, 64, 109, **29**
hyena 56

ibis 117
incense 33, 46
Isis 76
Islam 4

jewellers 33, 49, 52

ka 6ff, 18, 22
Karnak 17, 45, 61, 67, 81, 84, 93, 109
key 104
Khôkha 2, 17, 57, 67, 71
king 31–2, 35, 54
kitchen 21

laundry 80, **93**
leatherworkers 33, 52
lector priest 9
lime carbonate 12
limestone 12
linen 10, 24, 92, 102
Lisht 24
loaves 81
lotus 7, 42, 46, 76
lutist 64
Luxor 1, 2, 93

Maʿet 109
mandrake 42, 45, 46, 81
market scene 66, 109
mastaba 17, 19
measuring rope 104
Medinet Habu 92, 107, 126
Memnon colossi 94, 97, 129
Memphis 17, 69, 110
metal, weighing of 35, 70, 72
metalwork 21, 33, 52, **27**
Middle Kingdom 40
military 33ff, 65
milk 9
mirror dance 18
monochrome decoration 81–2
Monthu 68, 90
mortuary temple of Ḥatshepsut 2, 20
mortuary temple of Ramesses III 67
mortuary temple of Sethos I 2, 17
mud plaster 12
mules 60
mummy 11, (medicinal) 92
mummy on couch 89
mummy pits 102, 104
musical instruments 28
musicians 45, 88, 161, **93**
Mut 80, 81
myrrh 33, 46

Naqâda II 17
neck rest 24
Nubia 47, 49
Nubians 33, 84
nurse 55, **85**
Nut 88

obelisks 35
offering 35, 46
office 14, 32ff, 54–5, 65
oil 10
Old Kingdom 40
Opening of the Mouth 41, 53, **11**, **12**
opium 47
Osiris 8–9, 36, 40, 57, 65, 66, 73, 75, 76, 81, 83, 84, 85, 87, 89, 110, **11**, **67**, **88**
Osiris-Wennūfer 35, 58
outline draughtsman 14
oxen 10

painting, technique of 12
paintings, attribution of 29–30
paint vehicle 14
'palace of Qurna' 2, 93
palette 104
papyrus plant 46
pattern book 14–5, 50
physician 35
pictures, significance of 6–7, 30
pigeons 76
pigments 13–4
pillar 11
pipe 50
plaster, reliefs cut in 13
ploughing 27, 50
pomegranate 80
poppy 46, 81
potters 33, 88
Predynastic Period 28
prince 55
Ptolemaic burials 90
pyramid 11, 19, 20, 30, 74, 76, 80, **61**

quails 61
Qurna 1ff, **6**
Qurnet Muraʿi 2, 47ff, 67, 79, 90, 92

Ramesseum 71
Rēʿ 9, 85
rebirth 30, 36, 37, 42ff, 64, 80, 85, 88
red colour 38
Rēʿ-Ḥarakhti 35, 80, 87, 89
restoration 4, 110
reward 63, 65, 70, 76, **50**
riverscapes 56
rock, quality of 11
Roman burials 91, 116

ṣaff tombs 19
Saite tombs 96
sandals 50, 81
Saqqara 17, 69, 114
sarcophagus 11
scarabs 24, 92
scenery 56
scent 44, 57–8
sculpting, technique of 12–3
Second Intermediate Period 28
sem-priest 9
Serapeum 115
serpent 78, 83, **51**, **66**
Seth 38
sexuality 43
Sheikh ʿAbd el-Qurna 2, 21, 49ff, 66ff, 89, 91, 109, 113, **5**, **7**
ships 35
similarity in tomb decoration 14–5, 50
sistra 46
size 12
slaughter house 21
slaughtering 18
sledge 81
Sokari 75
solar cycle 16, 80
soldiers 50, **41**
sowing 27
spices 47
spinning 21
stables 21
stick 81
stone vessels, reliefs reused as 21
street 69
sun court 84–5, 88
sun's disc 51
swallow 7, 83
sycomore 11, 24, 71

Syrians 33, 59, **39**

tablet with hieroglyphs 77, 102, **65**
Thoth 83
threshing ground 27, 39, 60
tilapia fish 36
tombs, cutting of 11ff
tombs, number of 15
tombs, unfinished 11
treasure 21
tree goddess 65, 69, 71, 72, 76, 80, **52**, **63**
tribute 33, 52, 65
trumpet 35
Truth 65
T-shaped tombs 29, 30, 35, 40, 51, 52, 55, 57, 66, 76, **23**

unguent cone 44
unguents 10, 47, 58
ushabti 89

Valley of the Kings 3, 79, 82, 96, 98, 100, 115, 123
varnish 14, 57, 114
vase of Amūn 75
vases 33
vintage 39
viticulture 65, 80, 89
vizier 33, 65, 70

weaving 21, 65, 119, **20**
weighing of metal 35, 70, 72
weighing the heart 69, 72
Western goddess 57
wigs 43, 44, 45, 47, 82, **17**, **34**
wine 45, 62, **95**
winnowing 27, 39
woodworkers 88
workshops 49, 52, 65, 69, 70, 72, **59**
wreath, golden 92

II Ancient names

ʿAḥmosi Nefertere 58, 65, 66, 72, 80, 114, **60**, **88**
Alexander 90
Amenemḥab (TT 85) 55–6, **26**, **47**
Amenemḥēt I 24
Amenemḥēt 27
Amenemōnet (TT 58) 67
Amenemōnet (TT 277) 67–8
Amenemōpet (TT 41) 68–9, 70, **55**
Amenemōpet (TT 276) 49, **29**
Amenemōpet (TT A18) 76–7, **65**
Amenḥotp (TT 58) 67
Amenḥotp 109
Amenophis I 58, 65, 66, 72, 74, 80, 83, 114, **60**
Amenophis II 14, 50, 52, 54, 55, 59
Amenophis III 50, 56, 57, 59, 65, 66, 67, 109, **24**
Amenophis IV 50–1, 52, 56, 57, 65
ʿAmethu (TT 83) 105
ʿAnkhḥor (TT 414) 88
Antef (king) 19, **16**
Antef (TT 155) 59, **3**
Antefoḳer (TT 60) 24ff, 113, **22**
Augustus 91
Ay 61

Dagi (TT 103) 21
Ḏḥutiḥotp (TT A16) 77–8, **51**, **66**, **67**, **102**

Epiphanius 92
Espekashuti (TT 312) 89

Ḥaremḥab (king) 61, 62–3, **50**
Ḥatshepsut (queen) 2, 20, 59, 89
Ḥatshepsut 59
Hekamaʿetrēʿ-Nakht (TT 222) 68, **54**
Hekanakhte 21
Ḥuy (TT 40) 47–8, 49, **39**
Ḥuy (TT 54) 66

Ibi (TT 36) 88
Iḥy (TT 186) 18–9
Imiseba (TT 65) 67, **80**
Inḥerkhaʿ (TT 359) 83, **70**
Ipi (TT 315) 21
Ipuky (TT 181) 57, 127, **98**
Ipuy (TT 217) 80
Ipy (TT C6) 114
Irinūfer (TT 290) 82, **69**

Kawit **7**
Kemsit 20
Ḳenamūn (TT 93) 116
Kenro (TT 54) 66–7
Khaʿ (TT 8) 47, 119, **38**
Khaʿbekhnet (TT 2) 81
Khaʿemḥēt (TT 57) 50, **24**, **30**
Kharuef (TT 192) 56, 126, 128
Khenti (TT 405) 19, 21, 27, **15**
Kynebu (TT 113) 110–1, **2**, **87**

Maya (TT 138) 119
Meketrēʿ (TT 280) 21, 27, 123–4, **18**, **19**, **20**, **97**
Menkheper 89
Menna (TT 69) 49, 50, 59, 87, 110
Mentuemsaf 91–2
Mentuḥotp II 19
Mentuḥotp 24, **21**
Merymaʿet (TT C4) 109ff, **85**, **86**
Merymosi (TT 338) 48–9, **40**
Meryt 119, **38**
Min (TT 109) 98
Montuemḥēt (TT 34) 85–6, **71**, **72**, **73**
Mutemwia 72
Mutirdis (TT 410) 88, **74**

Nakht (TT 52) 49, 50, 59, 100, 116, **94**
Nakht (TT 161) 59, 111–2, **37**, **88**, **89**, **92**
Nakhtamūn (TT 341) 71, **57**
Nebamūn (TT 17) 59
Nebamūn (TT 65) 67
Nebamūn (TT 149) 117
Nebamūn (TT 181) 57, 127, **98**
Nebamūn 59, **35**, **49**
Nebwenenef (TT 157) 76
Neferḥotep (TT 49) 61–2
Neferḥotep (TT 50) 62, 102, **50**
Neferḥotep (TT A5) 98, 103
Neferronpet (TT 178) 71–2, **58**, **59**
Nefersekheru (TT 296) 73, **60**
Niay (TT 286) 76, **64**
Nitocris 88
Nofru 20, 27

Pabasa (TT 279) 88–9
Paḥeri 14ff, 30
Pairi (TT 139) 50, **11**, **33**
Paneḥesy (TT 16) 74–5, **62**, **63**
Parennūfer (TT 188) 57
Paser (TT 106) 69–70
Phoibammon 92
Piay (TT 263) 70, **56**
Psammetikos I 88
Puyemrēʿ (TT 39) 57, 98

Ramesses I 63
Ramesses II 70, 71, 76
Ramesses III 76, 83
Ramesses IV 83
Ramesses IX 67
Raʿmosi (TT 55) 50ff, 56, 63, 116, **42**, **43**
Raʿmosi (TT 132) 89
Raya (TT 159) 76
Rekhmirēʿ (TT 100) 52ff, 87, 116, **44**, **100**

Sebkemsaf 117
Sebkḥotp (TT 63) 113
Senenrēʿ (TT 246) 119
Senet 26ff
Senioḳer 19
Sennezem (TT 1) 80–1, 119
Sennūfer (TT 96) 53, 99, **45**, **46**
Sesostris I 24
Sethos I 69, 70, 71
Sheshonk (TT 27) 90, **76**
Strabo 93

Tetiky (TT 15) 58
Teye 56, 67, 126
Thonūfer (TT 158) 76, **52**
Trajan 92

Tutʿankhamūn 47, 54, 61, 63, 119, 123, **45**
Tuthmosis I 71, 79
Tuthmosis III 14, 27, 38, 52, 55, 57, 59, 105, 117
Tuthmosis IV 46, 57, 59, 113, 114

Unasʿankh (TT 413) 19
Userḥēt (TT 51) 70–1
Userḥēt (TT 56) 49–50, **41**
Userḥēt (TT A17) 78–9, **68**

Waḥ 22–3, 124
Wensu (TT A4) 14ff, 30, 59, 99, 103, 109, **84**

III Modern names

d'Athanasi, G. ('Yanni') 100, 102, 103, 104, 107, 109, 110
Atkins, S. 100

Bankes, W. J. 101–2, **81**, **82**
Baud, M. 130
Beechey, H. W. 100
Belzoni, G. B. 100
Bruce, J. 96
Bruyère, B. 125
Burton, H. 123, 124
Burton, J. 106ff, 125, **55**

Cailliaud, F. 103
Carnarvon, Lord 119
Carter, H. 119, 120, 123, 126
Champollion, J. F. 105, 107ff

Davies, Nina de Garis 122ff
Davies, Norman de Garis 27, 122ff
Denon, D. V. 98, **80**
Drioton, E. 126
Drovetti, B. 100, 101

Elgin, Lord 99
Emery, W. B. 120
Engelbach, R. 125

Fakhry, A. 126, 127
Fathy, H. 129
Felix, O. 110
Foucart, G. 126

Hamilton, W. R. 99, 109
Hay, R. 78, 106ff, 122, 123, 125, **2**, **3**, **10**, **16**, **39**, **50**, **51**, **53**, **65**, **66**, **67**, **76**, **84**, **87**, **88**, **102**
Hermann, A. 130

Irby, C. L. 100, 102

Jomard, E. F. 98

Keimer, L. 126

Lepsius, R. 113ff, 116, 125, **92**, **93**

Mackay, E. 120, 127
Málek, J. 125
Mangles, J. 100, 102
Mariette, A. 115
Mekhitarian, A. 130
Mohammed Ali 99, 106, 113, 114
Mond, R. 120–1, **96**
de Montulé, E. 99
Moss, R. L. B. 125

Napoleon 97–8
Newberry, P. E. 116, 117, 121
Norden, F. L. 93–5
Northampton (5th), Marquis of 116

Passalacqua, J. 24, 104, 113, **21**
Petrie, W. M. F. 117–9
Pococke, R. 95–6, **79**
Porter, B. 125
Prinsep, W. **6**
Prisse d'Avennes 112–3, **90**
Prudhoe, Lord 110

Rhind, A. H. 16, 115–6, **77**, **78**, **93**
Ripauld, L. M. 98
Rosellini, I. 107ff
Rustafjaell, R. de 117, 119ff

Saleh, M. 110
Salt, H. 100, 101, 103, 107, 109, **93**
Säve-Söderbergh, T. 130
Schiaparelli, E. 119
Schott, S. 126
Sicard, C. 93
Sonnini, C. S. 96–7
Spiegelberg, W. 116, 117
Steindorff, G. 130
Straton, J. 100, 101, 102, **81**
Strudwick, N. and H. 130

Tytus, R. de Pester 122

Weigall, A. 120ff
Wild, J. W. 113
Wilkinson, J. G. 104ff, 125, **28**, **83**, **93**
Winlock, H. E. 123ff, **97**
Wolf, W. 130

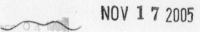